# DESIGNING for the TABLE

# DESIGNING for the TABLE

## Decorative and Functional Products

### MICHAEL WOLK

**Library of Applied Design**

*An Imprint of*

PBC INTERNATIONAL, INC. ◆ NEW YORK

Distributor to the book trade in the United States and Canada:

Rizzoli International Publications Inc.
300 Park Avenue South
New York, NY 10010

Distributor to the art trade in the United States and Canada:

PBC International, Inc.
One School Street
Glen Cove, NY 11542
1-800-527-2826
Fax 516-676-2738

Distributed throughout the rest of the world:

Hearst Books International
1350 Avenue of the Americas
New York, NY 10019

Library of Congress Cataloging-in-Publication Data

Wolk, Michael, 1951–
        Designing for the table: decorative and functional products / by
Michael Wolk.
            p.          cm.
        Includes index.
        ISBN 0-86636-177-4
        1. Tableware.    2. Glassware.    3. Porcelain.    I. Title.
TX877.W65    1992
642'.7--dc20                                                                91-43027
                                                                                    CIP

CAVEAT—Information in this text is believed accurate, and will pose no problem for the student
or casual reader. However, the author was often constrained by information contained in signed
release forms, information that could have been in error or not included at all. Any
misinformation (or lack of information) is the result of failure in these attestations. The author
has done whatever is possible to insure accuracy.

Color separation, printing and binding by
Toppan Printing Co. (H.K.) Ltd. Hong Kong

Typography by
TypeLink, Inc.

10 9 8 7 6 5 4 3 2 1

# ACKNOWLEDGMENTS

My thanks to Kevin Clark for inviting me to author *Designing for the Table* and to the entire PBC staff for their assistance and professionalism throughout the project. Together, I believe we have created a book you can both enjoy and turn to as a resource for years to come.

I must also acknowledge and thank my own staff, Lourdes Fernandez, Susan Halpern, and Glenda Herzog. Their talents and dedication to our other design projects allowed me the time and peace of mind needed to search through thousands of photographs to discover the unique and beautiful designs you'll see throughout these pages.

Finally and certainly most essentially, I want to thank all the artists, designers and photographers whose work is featured here. This book would not exist were it not for their imagination and creativity.

Dedicated to my wife Henri and our son Hunter, my special family.

# CONTENTS

*Christmas Rose Fine Bone China,*
*designed and manufactured by*
*Spode.*

# FOREWORD

## PEOPLE AND TABLETOP—PERFECT TOGETHER

**By Steven G. Changaris, CAE**
*Executive Director*
*National Tabletop Association*

Whether people gather for an exquisitely prepared meal in a fine restaurant or are called to the table by Mom, they share a unique and common experience. Before sampling the cuisine, their senses of sight and touch take control as they connect with the elements of the table setting laid before them. Impressions range from the regular and usual to the atypical and different. Feelings well up inside and immediately bring a mix of sensations—comfort, anticipation, fellowship, love, thankfulness and more. The enjoyment of the dining experience is indelibly shaped by the visual and tactile impressions created by the stemware, flatware, dishware, serving pieces and tabletop accessories gracing their table.

Tabletop manufacturers are constantly being challenged by consumers in an increasingly complex and global marketplace. Typically, our manufacturers need to be creative, traditional, futuristic and trendy. Yet, they are always sensitive to the consumer's often fickle interest in balancing design with functionality in tabletop products. Tabletop manufacturers, by meeting the challenges of today's marketplace, continue to uniquely position their products to be a force in our lives now and into the future.

The sum of the modern tabletop experience is definitely more than just pieces of tabletop. The real sum blends diverse elements: the basic human need to eat; an array of raw materials from silica to metal; various design influences which range from formal, casual, seasonal and traditional. And, when all combined, the experience reflects the personal expression of the host or hostess. Like people or the intricacies of a snowflake, no two tabletop settings are the same.

The editor who brings this book to you has done a wonderful job in researching tabletop. *Designing for the Table* presents a most contemporary and up-to-date view of tabletop. This book gives our imaginations a jump start on tabletop's future by clearly showing us where we've been and where we are today.

*The National Tabletop Association was formed in the mid 1980s by the diverse interests composing the tabletop industry, ranging from manufacturers of dinnerware, stemware and flatware to industry publications and allied interests.*

**National Tabletop Association Officers**

PRESIDENT
Gary Moreau
*President and CEO, Oneida*
VICE PRESIDENT
Ken Marvel
*President, Fitz & Floyd*
SECRETARY
Bill Simpson
*President, Pfaltzgraff Co.*

# NEW TRADITIONS IN TABLETOP DESIGN— A GALLERY OWNER'S PERSPECTIVE

By Deborah Farber-Isaacson
*Co-owner, Mindscape Gallery*

*Tradition.* There's a word just brimming with associations—cultural, familial, historical, personal. We think of tabletop traditions in terms of hospitality, the kind that nurtures and warms us, at small private gatherings or state dinners steeped in ceremony. The very styles that epitomize the applied decorative arts, including today's functional tabletop designs, are based on traditions—the continuation of a cherished ritual, the charming aesthetic of a treasured heirloom. But tradition is a very large concept, big enough to accommodate both our contemporary lifestyles and our appreciation of time-honored qualities such as graciousness and beauty. Clearly there is room for a diversity of tastes—of forms, periods, materials and styles. Most especially, there is room for individuality.

Taste, as I've come to realize after nearly two decades of marketing contemporary art and functional craft objects, is a multi-dimensional concept in its own right; it glitters with facets too numerous to count. In fact, our aesthetic preferences are every bit as complex and wide-ranging as our interests; we appreciate a lot of different designs for a lot of different reasons.

In a field as broad as tabletop design, which encompasses a segment of the contemporary craft industry, finding things to like is as easy as setting the table. Are you consistently drawn to the sparkle of handblown crystal? Do you just have to smile at the brightly enameled colors encased within a fused glass plate? Does your hand fit perfectly around the porcelain mug that holds your morning coffee? Maybe it's an artist's wit that appeals to you as you light the candle in a sculpted metal candle holder. Or perhaps it's your curiosity that's engaged by a process as rich in spirit and centuries-old philosophy as raku ceramics.

The world of tabletop design is so great that the selection of available art forms is limitless. It's as wide open as our imaginations permit and as inspiring as the talents that design and create what we think of as art.

At Mindscape Gallery, collectors of tabletop ware tend to be collectors of art forms in general, often viewing these products as potential additions to their collections. Not only do they combine one-of-a-kind crafts with commercially manufactured pieces, but they add antiques, a dash of primitive, a touch of glitz, or anything else that may capture their fancies. They may use their tables to display the works of many different artists, or to show variations on a favorite theme. There are artichoke and tulip collectors, and aficionados of frogs and unicorns in every layer of society. The charm, in every case, lies in the diversity displayed.

There is appeal, as well, in the endless variations to be found in things made by hand. A set of wheel-thrown porcelain bowls is guaranteed to vary in size. The glazes will differ from piece to piece, depending upon where things were placed in the kiln during firing. Bubbles or seeds appear in even the finest studio-blown glass. What we think of as flaws in ware produced under strict factory control may be viewed as desirable when the object is made by an artist. Collectors don't simply forgive such inconsistencies. They actively enjoy them.

The accent on individuality, which collectors appreciate and use so deftly, clearly begins with the maker. Tabletop products come not only in all kinds of styles, but with all kinds of intentions. Some are down-home utilitarian; others are elegant, or make daring design statements. Some are whimsical; others represent unique aesthetic perspectives. Some push their materials, representing advances in technology, or rare skill and craftsmanship. While some pieces blend harmoniously on the table, others nearly shout for attention.

There is, in addition, a function to each. Art critics, though not unanimously, generally acknowledge that art may now reside on the table, not simply on pedestals or within frames on the wall. If a critic is especially open-minded, an art form may hold soup or serve salad. It may pour tea or decant wine.

It is the design-minded public, however—hosts and diners, collectors and their guests—who have discovered an even greater truth about tabletop design. There is a unique pleasure to be found in using art, in interacting with it and incorporating it into our lives. It's an experience that's even better when we share it with friends and family across the table. That, too, is surely a tradition worth honoring.

*Deborah Farber-Isaacson is a professional craft advocate, author and co-owner of Mindscape Gallery, located in the Chicago area suburb of Evanston, Illinois. Established in 1974, Mindscape is one of the oldest and largest craft galleries in the United States, representing over 350 contemporary American artists.*

# INTRODUCTION

In the 1920s, the French Surrealist poet André Breton predicted "the distinction between art and life, so long held to be necessary, will be contested and will conclude with its being canceled out in principle." Seventy years later, this prediction is holding true in virtually every aspect of everyday life. The distinction between design and function, between art and utility, has given way to a sensibility in which there are no longer any firm barriers between aesthetics and practicality.

Historically in this country as in most of the Western world, artists pursued personal expression in the traditional art mediums of painting, drawing and sculpture. Their work was considered to exist on a wholly different plane than the work of craftsmen and artisans, who were making objects to fulfill the functional needs of their clients. This distinction between fine art and craft did not exist in other cultures, namely the Far Eastern cultures of Japan and China as well as primitive societies. For tribal people and the highly advanced Eastern civilizations, utilitarian objects held a very high place in the social value system. Japanese tea sets, for example, have ramifications which extend far beyond the act of drinking tea. They hold ritualistic and aesthetic significance which transcends pure functionality.

The work in this book demonstrates the variety of ways in which utilitarian objects transcend their function. Each serves in practical ways, and in more profound ways as well. They act as a kind of mirror, which reflects an image of ourselves and the quality of our daily existence. In many cases, these objects offer deeply meaningful commentaries on the social significance of being alive—of breaking bread, sharing a meal, engaging in social interaction.

Just as important, these objects return aesthetics to the world of daily life. They offer a more humanistic perspective on existence. Most are tactile as well as visual, offering their owners a level of enjoyment which is at once comforting and thought provoking. According to *Metropolitan Home,* design has become a social force, with the power to help us heal and to connect to one another and to the universe. Design-conscious objects serve a deep-rooted function by forging a link between ourselves and our environment. In this respect, design isn't simply about how things look, but about how things feel and the way they work.

Often, objects developed by corporate marketing divisions lack the substance of true design, because they lack a spiritual core. Aesthetics is, in its essence, a form of magic. When the cavemen painted their walls, they weren't merely engaging in decoration: they were practicing one of the basic arts of survival. The objects presented in this book display the same potent force to charm us, to console us, and to enrich our lives with a sensual form of meaning. Insofar as the human soul still requires a connection beyond itself, the objects shown here are the most potent form of modern magic that we know.

—Michael Wolk

*Table vignette, with antique and contemporary carved wooden accessories, designed by Ton Luyk.*

*Photo: Iran Issa-Khan*

# CHAPTER ONE

## Dishware

*Beaufort Fine Bone China, designed and manufactured by Spode.*

PRODUCT
**Olmec Series:**
**Dinnerware and Vase**
DESIGNER
**Ann Morhauser**
MANUFACTURER
**Annieglass Studio, Santa Cruz,**
**California**
PHOTOGRAPHER
**Viktor Budnic**

Frosted glass Olmec dinnerware repeats an image derived from the Olmec stone ruin in Mitla, Mexico. The plates are available in consecutive sizes with pattern/ground reversals. Vases are hand blown in Czechoslovakia and sandblasted by Annieglass.

PRODUCT
**Roman Antique Dinnerware**
DESIGNER
**Ann Morhauser**
MANUFACTURER
**Annieglass Studio, Santa Cruz, California**
PHOTOGRAPHER
**Viktor Budnic**

Rich, elegant Roman antique glass dinnerware hand painted with 24 karat gold and platinum bands. These circles of glass are kiln-fired to 1400° over hand-crafted molds to give the glass its distinctive "brushstroke" surfaces.

PRODUCT
**Petro Dinnerware**
DESIGNER
**Ann Morhauser**
MANUFACTURER
**Annieglass Studio, Santa Cruz, California**
PHOTOGRAPHER
**Viktor Budnic**

Images derived from cattle brands, graffiti and petroglyphs decorate this timeless slumped glass dinnerware.

PRODUCT
**Century Dinnerware,**
**Flatware, Crystal**
DESIGNER
**Tapio Wirkkala, K.G. Hansen,**
**Michael Boehm**
MANUFACTURER
**Rosenthal, Germany**

The smooth texture of Century White's porcelain was inspired by the sea urchin. An unusual combination of materials, silver and porcelain, distinguishes Century flatware. The ornamental relief on Century crystal's slender stems not only combines ease of grip with visual appeal but also complements the relief pattern of the porcelain.

*Available through Rosenthal Design Showroom, Dania, Florida.*

PRODUCT
**Suomi, White Dinnerware**
DESIGNER
**Timo Sarpaneva**
MANUFACTURER
**Rosenthal, Germany**

Finnish designer Timo Sarpaneva hand carved each piece of Suomi in wood before putting it in production. The soft shape and satin finish of the service reminds the artist of a river pebble worn smooth by the waters of time.

*Available through Rosenthal Design Showroom, Dania, Florida*

PRODUCT
**Mythos Dinnerware/Fabula Flatware**
DESIGNER
**Paul Wunderlich**
MANUFACTURER
**Rosenthal, Germany**

The feather motif on Paul Wunderlich's elegant Mythos dinnerware inspired the luxurious Fabula flatware collection. The feather can be found on the cutlery where it has been incorporated on the handles.

*Available through Rosenthal Design Showroom, Dania, Florida*

PRODUCT
**Mythos Dinnerware**
DESIGNER
**Paul Wunderlich**
MANUFACTURER
**Rosenthal, Germany**

Inspired by the legend of
Icarus, each piece of this
service features the fine
relief of feathers, with a
wing-like relief around
the oval plates and
"sculpted" feathers on
the lids of the pots.

*Available through Rosenthal Design
Showroom, Dania, Florida*

PRODUCT
**Polygon White Gourmet
Dinnerware**
DESIGNER
**Tapio Wirkkala**
MANUFACTURER
**Rosenthal, Germany**

The contrasting angular
and round surfaces of
Polygon create an inter-
esting light and shadow
effect. Handles on Poly-
gon pieces are designed
so that fingers do not
touch the hot pot.

*Available through Rosenthal Design
Showroom, Dania, Florida*

PRODUCT
**Cupola Strada Dinnerware**
DESIGNER
**Mario Bellini/Yang**
MANUFACTURER
**Rosenthal, Germany**

Cupola Strada combines Mario Bellini's shape with Yang's bold graphics. This design off-sets black with white, breaks continuous lines with areas of charcoal grey, divides up whole surfaces and links one small detail with another.

*Available through Rosenthal Design Showroom, Dania, Florida*

PRODUCT
**Mesa Dinnerware**
DESIGNER
**Kathleen Wills**
MANUFACTURER
**Dansk International Designs Ltd.**

Inspired by the interplay between the sea, the sky and sunwashed sand, Kathleen Wills created this collection in high-fired stoneware, in vibrant colors. Hand-crafted qualities are revealed in the thick, high-sided plate shape, the rich glazes, and the hand painted edge. Mesa is available in five colors: blue sky, white sand, turquoise, terra-cotta, and black.

PRODUCT
**Albertine**
DESIGNER
**Borek Sipek**
MANUFACTURER
**Driade**

White and blue porcelain
breakfast service with
plate, egg-cup and
teacup.

*Available through Stilnovo, Coral Gables,
Florida*

PRODUCT
**Cupola Fiorella Dinnerware**
DESIGNER
**Mario Bellini/Gisela Muller-
Behrendt**
MANUFACTURER
**Rosenthal, Germany**

Cupola uses the rich,
classical color of cobalt
blue and fine line of 22
karat gold on a modern,
floral pattern.

*Available through Rosenthal Design
Showroom, Dania, Florida*

PRODUCT
**Mosaic Dinnerware**
DESIGNER
**Victoria Rush Morrison**
MANUFACTURER
**Dansk International Designs Ltd.**

Mosaic dinnerware interprets an ancient art form in three patterns: tile, flower and wave. The designer hand laid miniature squares of colored tiles to each of the shapes and forms, expressing in exacting detail the feel of the mosaics of the Mediterranean.

PRODUCT
**Tiffany Tablesettings**
**Collection: "Century"**
DESIGNER
**Tiffany & Co.**
MANUFACTURER
**Tiffany & Co.**

"Century" china features a "stepped" band of refined greys reminiscent of the contours of Tiffany's "Century" flatware pattern. The sleek flatware typifies the Art Deco style and was introduced in 1937 to commemorate the firm's 100th anniversary.

PRODUCT
**"Madison Avenue"**
DESIGNER
**Paloma Picasso**
MANUFACTURER
**Villeroy & Boch**

A new collection of bone china dinnerware, "Madison Avenue" has a bas relief border detail that resembles a furled fabric. The texture is given greater definition by the gold outline and shading that fluidly follows the folds.

PRODUCT
**Trellis Dinnerware**
DESIGNERS
**David Tisdale and Judy Smilow**
MANUFACTURER
**Dansk International Designs Ltd.**

This design is inspired by the leaf covered trellis of country cottages of past and present. The pattern is based on a subtle contrast of white on white blended with the soft but clean colors of its rambling rim. Available in white, delft blue, mint and rose.

PRODUCT
**Quiltings Dinnerware**
DESIGNER
**Pattern by Victoria Rush Morrison**
**Form by Niels Refsgaard**
MANUFACTURER
**Dansk International Designs Ltd.**

Made of the finest European porcelain, Quiltings Dinnerware is based on the artwork of Amish Quiltmakers and reflects the dazzling colors and intricate stitchwork associated with Amish culture.

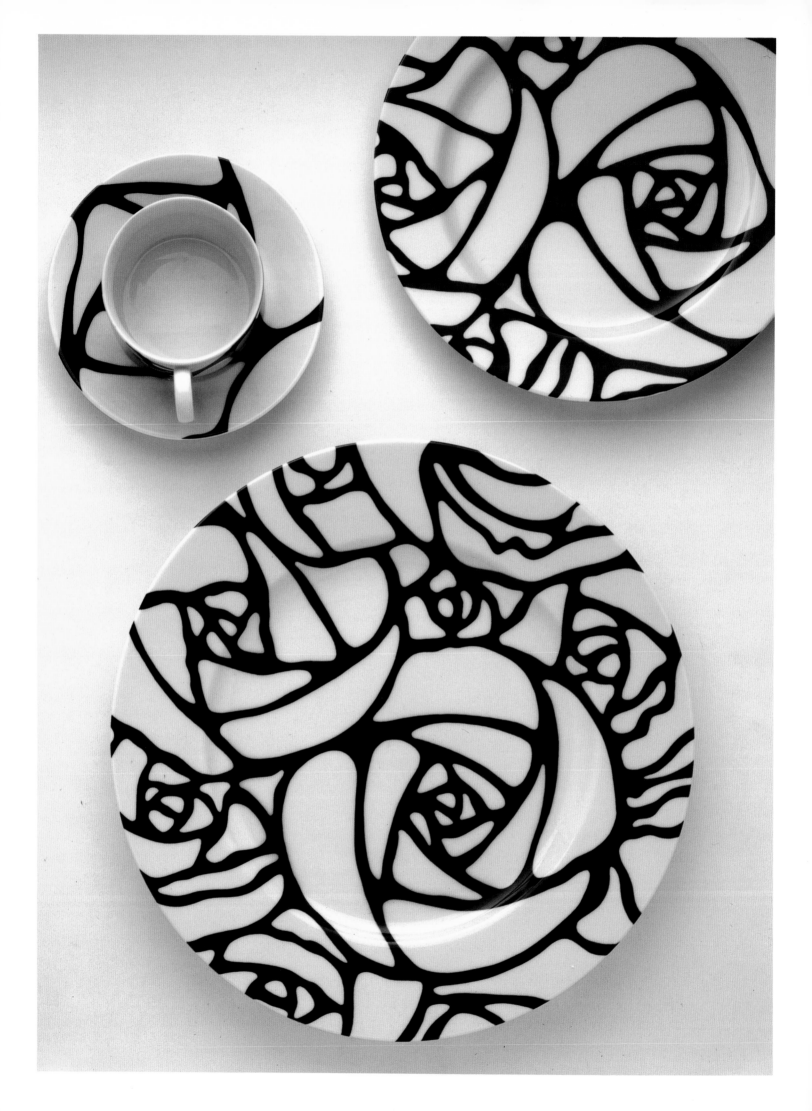

PRODUCT
**"Rose" Plates**
DESIGNER
**Frederic Schwartz,
Anderson/Schwartz Architects**
MANUFACTURER
**Swid Powell**
PHOTOGRAPHER
**Steve Moore**

Inspired by Japanese woodcuts and the Viennese Secessionist designer Kolo Moser, the "Rose" plates for Swid Powell reflect an interest in nature and ecology. A field of abstract white roses on a black background is symbolic landscape drawn from nature. The design, like nature itself, is complex and elegant, simple and beautiful.

PRODUCT
**"Morning Glory" Plates**
DESIGNER
**Frederic Schwartz**
MANUFACTURER
**Swid Powell**

"Morning Glory" plates were inspired by 19th century wood engravings of "Leaves and Flowers from Nature," found in Owen Jones *The Grammar of Ornament.* Graphically colored blue and yellow flowers seem to float above a black and white, realistic field of petals drawn with pen and ink. The design set includes a cup and saucer, soup bowl, dessert and dinner plate.

PRODUCT
**"Leaves" Plate**
DESIGNER
**Frederic Schwartz,
Anderson/Schwartz Architects
and Monika Banks**
PHOTOGRAPHER
**Steve Moore**

The "Leaves" plate, designed with Monica Banks for the Parkside restaurant in Atlanta, is inspired by fallen leaves from the trees in the park. The leaves are reproduced full size as a natural and varied border on the plates. Magnolia, gingko, dogwood, maple, linden and oak leaves dance elegantly around the plate's edge; a reminder of their simple and contrasting beauty.

*Available through ASAP, New York*

PRODUCT
**"Mikuni" Tableware 1** *(left)*
**"Mikuni" Tableware 2** *(below)*
DESIGNER
**Douglas Doolittle**
MANUFACTURER
**Noritake**
PHOTOGRAPHER
**Mizukoshi**

Bone china display plates
designed for hotel use.

PRODUCT
**Terra-Triangle with Cup and
Leaf Saucer**
DESIGNERS
**Teraki/Bisson
Romulus Craft**
MANUFACTURER
**Teraki/Bisson
Romulus Craft**

This versatile porcelain tableware includes: a terra color 11-inch triangular slab with black oxide slip; a leaf pattern saucer, and a demitasse cup with black oxide foot. Variations are also available—the triangle in black with a white inset, the saucer in plain white or black oxide.

PRODUCT
**Bowl with Saki Cups**
DESIGNERS
**Teraki/Bisson
Romulus Craft**
MANUFACTURER
**Teraki/Bisson
Romulus Craft**
PHOTOGRAPHER
**Romulus Craft**

Thick slab bowl with five saki cups in black and white porcelain.

PRODUCT
**Cup, "Pillow" Saucer**
**Slab, Ring Plate**
**Square Saki Cups**
DESIGNERS
**Teraki/Bisson**
**Romulus Craft**
MANUFACTURER
**Teraki/Bisson**
**Romulus Craft**
PHOTOGRAPHER
**Romulus Craft**

This distinctive black and white porcelain tableware features a white square attached to a black oxide ring, white cup with clear glaze, and textured black oxide saucer. The square saki cups in textured black oxide are also available in white with a black oxide band.

PRODUCT
**Plate**
DESIGNERS
**Teraki/Bisson**
**Romulus Craft**
MANUFACTURER
**Teraki/Bisson**
**Romulus Craft**
PHOTOGRAPHER
**Romulus Craft**

Terra-cotta plate torched with rings.

PRODUCT
**Dinnerware**
DESIGNER
**Marek Cecula**
MANUFACTURER
**Marek Cecula/Contemporary Porcelain**
PHOTOGRAPHER
**Bill Waltzer**

Slip cast porcelain dinnerware set in mixed colors: apple green, yellow, cobalt and rose. The black edge adds definition, visually unifying the diverse pieces.

PRODUCT
**Fruits**
DESIGNER
**William McGrath**
MANUFACTURER
**Crystallery de Genesis**

Place setting in hand-made glass with colorful medley of fresh fruit motif: dinner plate, 11″; bread and butter, 7″; salad, 9″; dessert dish, 7″; cup, 4″.

*Available through Crystallery de Genesis, Rochester, New York*

PRODUCT
**Rain Forest**
DESIGNER
**William McGrath**
MANUFACTURER
**Crystallery de Genesis**

Handmade glass plates from Crystallery de Genesis fuse hundreds of shades of colored glass into beautiful paintings permanently encased in crystal clear glass. The colors are powdered and lightly brushed on, while detail is accomplished by scraffito and brush stroke. Each piece is unique.

*Available through Crystallery de Genesis, Rochester, New York*

PRODUCT
**Century New Wave Dinnerware**
DESIGNER
**Dorothy Hafner**
MANUFACTURER
**Rosenthal, Germany**

The honeycomb texture of this porcelain created by Finnish artist Tapio Wirkkala is 30 percent more translucent than any other high quality dinnerware. Dorothy Hafner's palette of pinks, blues, greens and yellows complements the porcelain's unique transparent quality.

*Available through Rosenthal Design Showroom, Dania, Florida*

PRODUCT
**Flash Dinnerware**
DESIGNER
**Dorothy Hafner**
MANUFACTURER
**Rosenthal, Germany**

Flash is bold, dynamic
and unusual in shape
and decoration. A fine ceramic, each piece is de-
signed to fulfill multiple
functions. It can be used
as a complete dinnerware
service or as a colorful
accent that adds excite-
ment to home
entertaining.

*Available through Rosenthal Design
Showroom, Dania, Florida*

PRODUCT
**"Siena"**
DESIGNER
**Robert Murray**
MANUFACTURER
**Manufactured in Sri Lanka**
PHOTOGRAPHER
**Oggetti**

Colorful hand-painted
ceramic dinnerware suit-
able for daily use, parties
and big buffets.

*Available through Oggetti, Miami, Florida*

PRODUCT
**Mardi Gras Series**
DESIGNER
**Wesley Dunn**
MANUFACTURER
**Wesley Dunn**
PHOTOGRAPHER
**Wesley Dunn**

Clear, strong bright colors characterize this festive series of hand thrown ceramic plates and bowls.

PRODUCT
**Plate Set: Flying Toast; Moroccan Room; Pink Candlesticks; Striped Chair**
DESIGNER
**Claudia DeMonte**
MANUFACTURER
**Jason McCoy, Inc.**
PHOTOGRAPHER
**Beth Phillips**

Set of four colorful Melamite country luncheon or dinner plates designed by fine artist Claudia DeMonte.

PRODUCT
**Salad/Dessert Plate**
DESIGNER
**Wesley Dunn**
MANUFACTURER
**Wesley Dunn**
PHOTOGRAPHER
**Wesley Dunn**

Featured in this tableset- ting is Wesley Dunn's hand thrown ceramic plate designed with a white spiral motif on a blue underglaze and ac- cented by randomly placed groupings of small black dots.

PRODUCT
**Salad Plate**
DESIGNER
**Wesley Dunn**
MANUFACTURER
**Wesley Dunn**
PHOTOGRAPHER
**Wesley Dunn**

A vibrant pastel under- glaze enhances the white spiral and border pattern on this large-size, hand thrown ceramic salad plate.

PRODUCT
**Magic Flute Sarastro**
DESIGN
**Bjorn Wiinblad**
MANUFACTURER
**Rosenthal, Germany**

The filigree raised relief on Magic Flute Sarasto is coated with 24 karat gold.

*Available through Rosenthal Design Showroom, Dania, Florida*

PRODUCT
**Magic Flute, Osiris Dinnerware**
DESIGNER
**Bjorn Wiinblad**
MANUFACTURER
**Rosenthal, Germany**

Poetry in porcelain, every piece of Magic Flute depicts a different scene from Mozart's last and greatest composition. On the reverse side of every plate, the libretto of the scene is handwritten in gold.

*Available through Rosenthal Design Showroom, Dania, Florida*

PRODUCT
**La Maison de l'Art Deco China, La Maison de Louis Cartier Sterling Silver, La Maison des Ballets Russes Stemware**
DESIGNER
**Les Maisons de Cartier**
MANUFACTURER
**Cartier**

The wonder of Egypt is recaptured in the drama of La Maison de L'Art Deco ivory dinnerware pattern. Regal 24 karat gold panthers are framed with geometric Art Deco motif accented by a hand enameled version of the Cartier cabochon sapphire. The stemware is recognized by a frosted motif around the cylindrical bowl, originally inspired by a curtain treatment from Diaghailev's Russian Ballet.

PRODUCT
**"Seven Seas" Sushi Plate**
DESIGNER
**Douglas Doolittle**
MANUFACTURER
**Morimoto**
PHOTOGRAPHER
**Mizukoshi**

The design for this sushi plate is a very subtle transmutation from a logo designed for a restaurant called "Seven Seas."

PRODUCT
**Royal Copenhagen Table Setting**
DESIGNER
**Royal Copenhagen Continental Flatware by Georg Jensen**
MANUFACTURER
**Royal Copenhagen, Georg Jensen**

The Blue Fluted, half-lace Royal Copenhagen dinner service is based on an ancient Chinese porcelain pattern and is still painted freehand. The graceful stemware is also by Royal Copenhagen. Sterling silver flatware is Georg Jensen's classic Continental pattern.

PRODUCT
**Shima Border Fine Bone China**
DESIGNER
**Spode**
MANUFACTURER
**Spode**

The open center in this popular pattern increases the impact of the beautiful Imari border, achieving a light, uncluttered look. Shima is versatile and mixes well with Consul Cobalt and other patterns.

PRODUCT
**Tiffany Tablesettings**
**Collection: "Chrysanthemum"**
DESIGNER
**Tiffany & Co.**
MANUFACTURER
**Tiffany & Co.**

"Chrysanthemum" china
is rendered in "Imari"
shades of cobalt blue,
russet, gold, and imperial
green. It is a striking
evolution of Tiffany's
"Chrysanthemum" flat-
ware, introduced in 1880.

PRODUCT
**Tiffany Tablesettings**
**Collection: "Audubon"**
DESIGNER
**Tiffany & Co.**
MANUFACTURER
**Tiffany & Co.**

"Audubon" china, with its
border of birds and flora,
is inspired by Tiffany's
"Audubon" flatware, a
pattern created in 1871.

PRODUCT
**Tiffany Tablesettings**
**Collection: "Hampton"**
DESIGNER
**Tiffany & Co.**
MANUFACTURER
**Tiffany & Co.**

"Hampton" china is inspired by Tiffany's "Hampton" flatware, a classically styled pattern patented in 1934. The dessert plate features an entwined gold tulip and rose, reminiscent of the flowers in Hampton Court Palace, the country home of English kings and queens.

PRODUCT
**VIP Cups and Saucers**
DESIGNER
**Royal Worcester**
MANUFACTURER
**Royal Worcester**

The VIP Cup and Saucer Collection is a series of over-sized cups and saucers in Fine Bone China and trimmed in 22 karat gold. The inside of each cup is inscribed to the "Very Important Person" while the outside is beautifully decorated with different scenes from the sporting world, including golf, tennis and fishing.

PRODUCT
**La Maison du Prince**
DESIGNER
**Les Maisons de Cartier**
MANUFACTURER
**Cartier**

La Maison du Prince reflects a mood of grandeur in china, crystal and flatware. The crystal is tulip-shaped with long, slim cuts of the bowl rising out of a deeply cut and gracefully contoured stem. The ornate china pattern reflects a "Neo-Renaissance" look with richly colored florals and lavish cornucopias of leaves, grapes and shells.

PRODUCT
**La Maison de Louis Cartier
China**
DESIGNER
**Les Maisons de Cartier**
MANUFACTURER
**Cartier**

The design for this china pattern is based on an elegant brooch from the Cartier archives. Whimsical leaping leopards are featured with bold, contrasting colors (black, red, green and gold) against a white background.

PRODUCT
**Delphi Fine Bone China**
DESIGNER
**Spode**
MANUFACTURER
**Spode**

Spode's Delphi pattern features a rich gold edge. It mixes and matches beautifully with many other patterns.

PRODUCT
**Lausanne Fine Bone China**
DESIGNER
**Spode**
MANUFACTURER
**Spode**

Lausanne is a new pattern that features a lovely powdered finish in a narrow band of rich Georgian blue accented with 24 karat gold.

PRODUCT
**Seville Fine Bone China**
DESIGNER
**Spode**
MANUFACTURER
**Spode**

Designed for the bridal market, Seville is distinguished by a warm terracotta border edged in 22 karat gold.

PRODUCT
**Tuscana Fine Bone China**
DESIGNER
**Spode**
MANUFACTURER
**Spode**

Designed for the bridal market, Tuscana features a powdered finish in a narrow band of deep green accented with 22 karat gold.

PRODUCT
**Marquis Fine Bone China**
DESIGNER
**Royal Worcester**
MANUFACTURER
**Royal Worcester**

A classic white pattern, Marquis has 22 karat gold feather gilding that highlights the shape's gracefulness and beauty.

PRODUCT
**Chatsworth Fine Bone China**
DESIGNER
**Spode**
MANUFACTURER
**Spode**

Designed for the bridal market, Chatsworth is a formal pattern in English Regency style, featuring gilded festoons on a wide inner cream band with an embellished teal blue border.

PRODUCT
**Brighton Fine Bone China**
DESIGNER
**Royal Worcester**
MANUFACTURER
**Royal Worcester**

A strong bridal pattern designed exclusively for the U.S. market, Brighton features a wide border swag of blue bows on the traditional Garrick shape.

PRODUCT
**Tiffany Tablesettings**
**Collection: "Shell & Thread"**
DESIGNER
**Tiffany & Co.**
MANUFACTURER
**Tiffany & Co.**

"Shell & Thread" china features a blue and white border of delicate shells interspersed with palmettes. The china echoes the motifs of Tiffany's "Shell & Thread" silver, the firm's most popular flatware since its introduction in 1905.

PRODUCT
**Diplomat Fine Bone China**
DESIGNER
**Royal Worcester**
MANUFACTURER
**Royal Worcester**

A beautiful color statement, Diplomat combines 22 karat gold feather gilding with a wide cobalt border.

PRODUCT
**Saratoga**
DESIGNER
**Floria Popovici McGuckian**
MANUFACTURER
**Pfaltzgraff Company**

A fresh floral pattern in
bone china with raised,
stylized mums in peach,
mauve and summer
green, trimmed with 22
karat gold.

PRODUCT
**Whitney**
DESIGNER
**Floria Popovici McGuckian**
MANUFACTURER
**Pfaltzgraff Company**

Delicate yet durable bone
china with roseblush and
soft aqua bouquets en-
circled by 22 karat gold.

PRODUCT
**Tiara Fine Bone China**
DESIGNER
**Spode**
MANUFACTURER
**Spode**

Done in the fluted Chelsea shape, Tiara recalls a charming Victorian pattern. Pale pink roses interplay with salmon button dahlias and baby blue forget-me-nots on a 22 karat gold border.

PRODUCT
**"Basket" Dinnerware**
DESIGNER
**Helen Von Boch**
MANUFACTURER
**Villeroy & Boch**

The "Basket" pattern from Villeroy & Boch is a classic design in dinnerware, popularized by the chefs who introduced nouvelle cuisine and favored for the dramatic framework it creates for food presentation.

PRODUCT
**Fairfield Porcelain**
DESIGNER
**Royal Worcester**
MANUFACTURER
**Royal Worcester**

Fairfield features bold,
fresh flowers on a white
porcelain background. A
strong bridal dinnerware
pattern, it coordinates
with Fairfield cookware.

PRODUCT
**Savoy Fine Bone China**
DESIGNER
**Spode**
MANUFACTURER
**Spode**

Savoy is a reproduction
of an 18th-century floral
pattern from the Spode
archives. A gold overlay
on a soft blue border dra-
matizes the Stafford
shape and frames the flo-
ral spray center.

PRODUCT
**Worcester Herbs Porcelain**
DESIGNER
**Royal Worcester**
MANUFACTURER
**Royal Worcester**

Worcester Herbs is a
charming pattern of bo-
tanical drawings of popu-
lar English herbs with a
Cotswold style flowered
border. All items are
freezer, oven, microwave,
and dishwasher safe.

PRODUCT
**Ashford Fine English
Porcelain**
DESIGNER
**Royal Worcester**
MANUFACTURER
**Royal Worcester**

This English country pat-
tern with a soft dusty
rose edging is microwave-
safe.

PRODUCT
**Chinese Garden Fine Bone China**
DESIGNER
**Royal Worcester**
MANUFACTURER
**Royal Worcester**

Inspired by Chinese designs, this lovely floral pattern features softly-colored chrysanthemums outlined with a tracery of 22 karat gold to give a delicate cloisonné effect.

PRODUCT
**Holly Ribbons Fine Bone China**
DESIGNER
**Royal Worcester**
MANUFACTURER
**Royal Worcester**

A formal holiday pattern appropriate in any setting, Holly Ribbons evokes Victorian charm with its interplay of silk ribbons and berried holly.

PRODUCT
**Golden Valley Fine Bone China**
DESIGNER
**Spode**
MANUFACTURER
**Spode**

A lavishly gilded pattern, Golden Valley is executed on the classic Stafford shape. The pattern features a fruit cluster encircled by a rich floral gold border.

PRODUCT
**"Vie Sauvage" Dinnerware**
DESIGNER
**Gero Trauth**
MANUFACTURER
**Villeroy & Boch**

Exotic birds and colorful forest scenes reveal Gero Trauth's artistry in this bone china dinnerware from Villeroy & Boch.

# CHAPTER TWO

## Flatware

PRODUCT
**Torun Flatware**
DESIGNER
**Vivianna Torun Bulow-Hube**
MANUFACTURER
**Dansk International Designs Ltd.**

Sleek and contemporary, Torun flatware is available in stainless and silverplate.

PRODUCT
**English Chippendale**
DESIGNER
**Reed & Barton**
MANUFACTURER
**Reed & Barton**

Graceful lines distinguish Reed & Barton's sterling silver flatware in the classic English Chippendale pattern.

PRODUCT
**Eighteenth Century**
DESIGNER
**Reed & Barton**
MANUFACTURER
**Reed & Barton**

Unique styling has made "Eighteenth Century" sterling silver flatware a contemporary classic and one of America's most revered patterns.

PRODUCT
**Country Charm**
DESIGNER
**Reed & Barton**
MANUFACTURER
**Reed & Barton**

The tasteful, delicate simplicity of "Country Charm" ensures an attractive tablesetting. Crafted from "Elite Silverplate," it provides the elegance of silverplate at a moderate price.

PRODUCT
**La Maison du Prince Silverplated Flatware**
DESIGNER
**Les Maisons de Cartier**
MANUFACTURER
**Cartier**

The *Prince* design is an understated "fiddle" shape in a continental size pattern, executed in heavy silverplate. The Cartier "rolling ring" and oval backstamp are rendered in elegant gold vermeil.

PRODUCT
**Crescendo/Golden Crescendo**
DESIGNER
**Reed & Barton**
MANUFACTURER
**Reed & Barton**

Crescendo and Golden
Crescendo are crafted
from the finest mainte-
nance-free 18/8 stainless
steel.

PRODUCT
**"Apollo"/"Apollo Gold"**
DESIGNER
**Reed & Barton**
MANUFACTURER
**Reed & Barton**

Perfect for a wide range of table settings, "Apollo" is a bold new design with classic lines. Made of 18/8 stainless steel, this pattern is also available in a variation, "Apollo Gold," accented with 24 karat gold.

PRODUCT
**Seafare/Golden Seafare**
DESIGNER
**Reed & Barton**
MANUFACTURER
**Reed & Barton**

Introduced in 1990, Seafare flatware is 18/8 stainless steel. Golden Seafare is accented with 24 karat gold.

PRODUCT
**"Agrigento"**
DESIGNER
**Paloma Picasso**
MANUFACTURER
**Villeroy & Boch**

"Agrigento's" detailed motif imitates a furled fabric with a carved tassel playfully ornamenting the top on both front and back. It is executed in a choice of 18/10 stainless steel, silverplate, or silverplate with 24 karat gold accents.

PRODUCT
**Woodwind**
DESIGNER
**Reed & Barton**
MANUFACTURER
**Reed & Barton**

The lustrous finish and rich detail of sterling silver enhance this timeless design.

PRODUCT
**"Bel Air" Elite Silverplate**
DESIGNER
**Reed & Barton**
MANUFACTURER
**Reed & Barton**

The delicate ornamentation of "Bel Air" silverplate complements both formal and casual tablesettings.

PRODUCT
**Ashmont/Golden Ashmont**
DESIGNER
**Reed & Barton**
MANUFACTURER
**Reed & Barton**

Impeccably crafted sterling silver, Ashmont is also available in a variation, Golden Ashmont, with a 24 karat gold accent.

PRODUCT
**Tangent**
DESIGNER
**Vivianna Torun Bulow-Hube**
MANUFACTURER
**Dansk International Designs
Ltd.**

Hot-forged and hand-polished flatware in the finest 18/8 stainless steel.

PRODUCT
**ALIX**
DESIGNER
**Borek Sipek**
MANUFACTURER
**Driade**

Finely designed, tapered silverplate flatware in an eight-piece place setting: table fork; fruit fork; tablespoon; dessert spoon; coffee spoon; table knife; fruit knife.

*Available through Stilnovo, Coral Gables, Florida*

PRODUCT
**Forks**
DESIGNER
**Michel Royston**
MANUFACTURER
**Michel Royston**
PHOTOGRAPHER
© **Tom Wachs**
Design © **Michel Royston**

Sculptural and utilitarian
hand-forged sterling sil-
ver forks from Hat Creek
Forge.

PRODUCT
**Sterling Flatware**
DESIGNER
**Michel Royston**
MANUFACTURER
**Michel Royston**
PHOTOGRAPHER
**Kathi Corder**

Each piece of Michel Royston's exquisite hand-forged sterling silver flatware achieves maximum strength from being worked on all sides. Custom-made stainless steel knife blades are joined to the sterling handles.

PRODUCT
**Composition Flatware**
DESIGNER
**Tapio Wirkkala**
MANUFACTURER
**Rosenthal, Germany**

This brushed steel flat-ware is comfortable to hold. The shape of the knife is based on the par-allelogram and can be used for cutting with minimal effort.

*Available through Rosenthal Design Showroom, Dania, Florida*

PRODUCT
**Sculptura Flatware**
DESIGNER
**Lino Sabattini**
MANUFACTURER
**Rosenthal, Germany**

Well balanced and per-fectly shaped, Sculptura silver flatware turns knives, forks and spoons into miniature works of art.

*Available through Rosenthal Design Showroom, Dania, Florida*

PRODUCT
**"Aura"**
DESIGNER
**Walter Storr**
MANUFACTURER
**Wilkens, Germany**

Created for Wilkens by
Walter Storr, "Aura" has
won numerous interna-
tional design awards. The
clean sculptural lines are
highlighted by pro-
portion and balance
achieved by skilled
craftsmanship. "Aura" is
manufactured from a
special combination of
chrome-nickel steel, an
alloy consisting of 18 percent chrome and 8 per-
cent nickel. Knife blades
are made of high carbon
steel.

*Distributed exclusively by Grainware.*

PRODUCT
**EXL Place Setting**
DESIGNER
**Robert Wilhite**
MANUFACTURER
**Bissell & Wilhite Co.**

Five-piece place setting
in 18/8 stainless steel
from Bissell & Wilhite's
EXL pattern.

PRODUCT
**Dialog Flatware**
DESIGNER
**Lino Sabbatini**
MANUFACTURER
**Rosenthal, Germany**

The thin, delicate handles of Dialog flatware are accented at their ends by a small sphere, lending an almost post-modern touch to this elegant flatware design.

*Available through Rosenthal Design Showroom, Dania, Florida*

PRODUCT
**"Twig Ware"**
DESIGNER
**Michael Aram**
MANUFACTURER
**Michael Aram**

Silver plated sand cast brass flatware and service sets, inspired from Nature.

*Available through Lewis Dolin, Inc.*

PRODUCT
**OBOR Flatware**
DESIGNER
**Susan Ewing,
INTERALIA/Design**
MANUFACTURER
**Susan Ewing,
INTERALIA/Design**
PHOTOGRAPHER
**Rick Potteiger**

Hand crafted five-piece
place setting in sterling
silver.

PRODUCT
**Sterling Silver Serving Pieces**
DESIGNER
**Michel Royston**
MANUFACTURER
**Michel Royston**
PHOTOGRAPHER
**Kathi Corder**

Hand-forged sterling silver serving pieces.

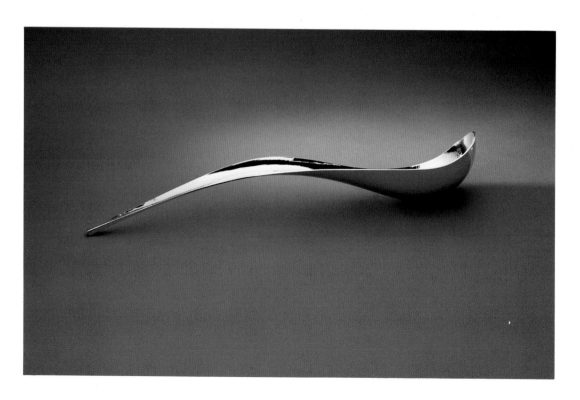

PRODUCT
**Creek Wash Ladle**
DESIGNER
**Michel Royston**
MANUFACTURER
**Michel Royston**
PHOTOGRAPHER
**© Tom Wachs**
**Design © Michel Royston**

Sculptural in appearance, this elegant sterling silver ladle is hand-forged.

PRODUCT
**Dessert Fork, Dessert Spoon,
Napkin Ring**
DESIGNER
**Robyn Nichols**
MANUFACTURER
**Robyn Nichols**
PHOTOGRAPHER
**Hollis Officer**

Nasturtium pattern sterling silver dessert fork, spoon and napkin ring, hand fabricated with forged handles.

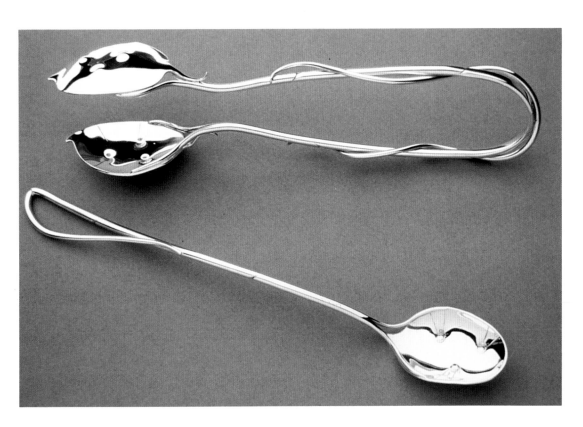

PRODUCT
**Ice Tongs, Ice Tea Spoon**
DESIGNER
**Robyn Nichols**
MANUFACTURER
**Robyn Nichols**
PHOTOGRAPHER
**Hollis Officer**

Fabricated sterling silver ice tongs (7"l) and ice tea spoon (8"l) with money plant motif.

PRODUCT
**Salad Servers**
DESIGNER
**Robyn Nichols**
MANUFACTURER
**Robyn Nichols**
PHOTOGRAPHER
**Hollis Officer**

Designed from nature, these sterling silver nasturtium leaf salad servers are hand fabricated. Sterling silver wire is used to create the leaf veins.

PRODUCT
**Hibiscus Beverage Ladle**
DESIGNER
**Robyn Nichols**
MANUFACTURER
**Robyn Nichols**
PHOTOGRAPHER
**Hollis Officer**

Sterling silver hibiscus beverage ladle with chased petals and hand formed pestle.

PRODUCT
**Water Grass Hors d'Oeuvre
Fork and Spreader**
DESIGNER
**Robyn Nichols**
MANUFACTURER
**Robyn Nichols**
PHOTOGRAPHER
**Hollis Officer**

Hand fabricated sterling
silver hors d'oeuvre fork
and spreader with water
grass motif.

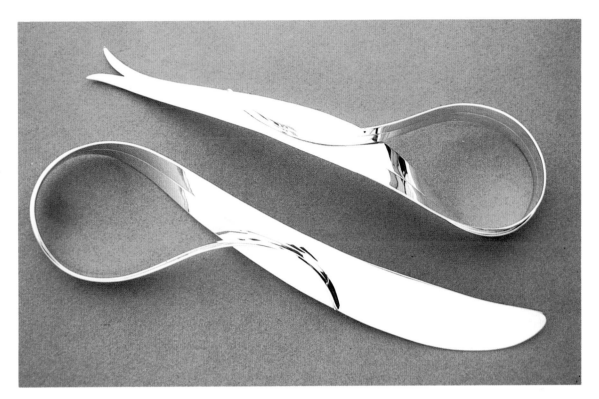

PRODUCT
**Salad Serving Set**
DESIGNER
**Michael Graves**
MANUFACTURER
**Swid Powell by Reed & Barton**

Michael Graves' silver-
plated salad serving set is
artfully decorated with a
floral motif.

PRODUCT
**Carving Set**
DESIGNER
**Robert Venturi**
MANUFACTURER
**Swid Powell by Reed & Barton**

Winner of the International Tabletop Award for design excellence, the Venturi Carving Set has silverplated handles and stainless steel blades and tines.

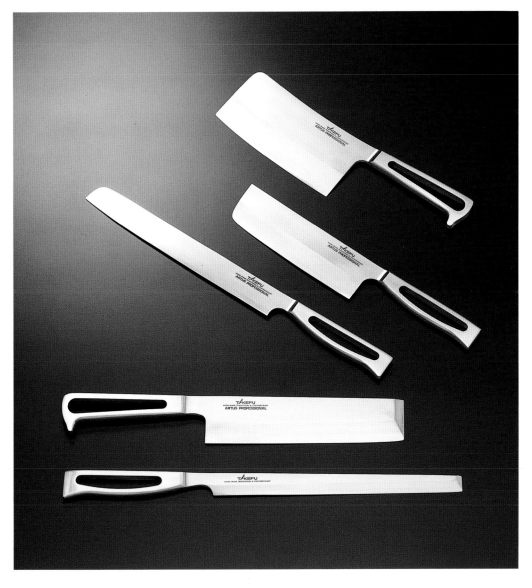

PRODUCT
**Takefu Knife Series**
DESIGNER
**Kazuo Kawasaki**
MANUFACTURER
**Takefu**

Functional and beautifully designed knives for carving, chopping and slicing, made from V-700 high-grade laminated stainless steel.

*Available through Gallery 91, New York.*

PRODUCT
**Dessert Serving Set**
DESIGNER
**David Palterer**
MANUFACTURER
**Swid Powell by Reed & Barton**

Crafted in the finest 18/8 stainless steel with ebony wood handles, David Palterer's Dessert Serving Set includes a graceful knife and server that gravitate to each other in a free flowing ensemble that is as pleasing to look at as it is to use.

PRODUCT
**Dessert Set**
DESIGNER
**Ettore Sottsass**
MANUFACTURER
**Swid Powell by Reed & Barton**

Elegant and witty, this ice cream scoop and pie server set with curved handles is hand-crafted of the highest quality 18/8 stainless steel.

PRODUCT
**EXL Serving Pieces**
DESIGNER
**Robert Wilhite**
MANUFACTURER
**Bissell & Wilhite Co.**

Sterling silver slotted
spoon, serving fork and
serving spoon in Bissell
& Wilhite's EXL pattern.

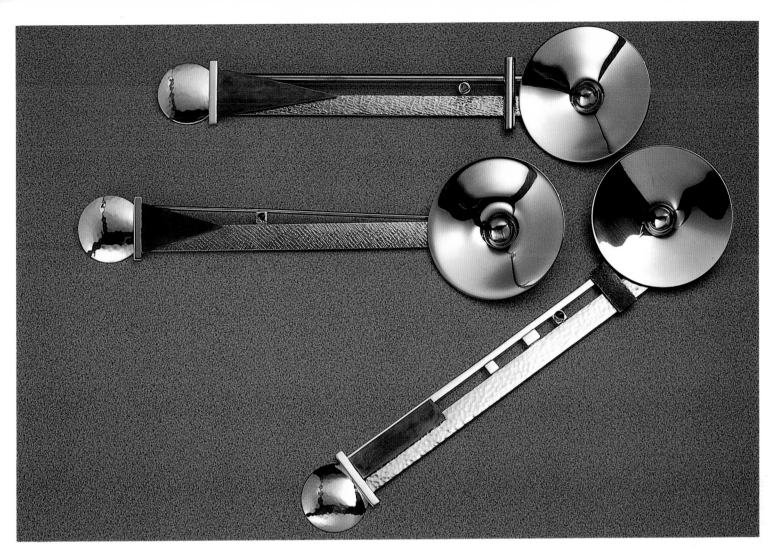

PRODUCT
**Serving Pieces**
DESIGNER
**Randy Stromsoe**
MANUFACTURER
**Randy Stromsoe, Stromsoe Studios**
PHOTOGRAPHERS
**Ron and Frank Bez**

Distinctive serving pieces combining polished pewter, sterling silver, copper, 14 karat gold and gem stones.

PRODUCT
**Serving Set**
DESIGNER
**Cynthia Eid**
MANUFACTURER
**Cynthia Eid**
PHOTOGRAPHER
**Cynthia Eid**

Forged sterling silver serving set.

# CHAPTER THREE

# Stemware and Barware

*Dining room tablescape and interiors designed by William L. Vernon of Richard Plumer Design, Miami, Florida.*

*Photo: Dan Forer*

PRODUCT
**Cupola Crystal**
DESIGNER
**Mario Bellini**
MANUFACTURER
**Rosenthal, Germany**

Made of full lead crystal,
Cupola is the world's first
twin-stemmed glassware.
Elegant enough for for-
mal dining, but sturdy
enough for daily use, Cu-
pola is a companion to
Rosenthal's matching
dinnerware service.

*Available through Rosenthal Design
Showroom, Dania, Florida*

PRODUCT
**Clermont Gold Stemware**
DESIGNER
**William E. Hoffer**
**W E H Design**
MANUFACTURER
**Gorham Inc.**

Gorham's Clermont Gold stemware designed by William E. Hoffer is part of Gorham's Masterpiece Stemware Collection. Hand banded in 24 karat gold, Clermont Gold is versatile in design and easily coordinates with a number of table settings.

PRODUCT
**"Ebony Dior"**
DESIGNER
**William E. Hoffer**
**W E H Design**
MANUFACTURER
**Christian Dior**

Black lead crystal and clear lead crystal with a decorative gold edge treatment, "Ebony Dior" stemware is available in four sizes: water, wine, great wine and champagne flute.

PRODUCT
**Enrico**
DESIGNER
**Borek Sipek**
MANUFACTURER
**Driade**

Exquisite crystal stemware designed by Borek Sipek reflects the spontaneous rhythms of nature. (White wine, red wine, water, liqueur, champagne)

*Available through Stilnovo, Coral Gables, Florida*

PRODUCT
**Trillium**
DESIGNER
**William E. Hoffer for Oneida Ltd.**
MANUFACTURER
**Dalzell Viking Glass**
PHOTOGRAPHER
**B.C. Design**

Casual stemware with an abstract three-repeat leaf motif, available in cobalt, peach, green, clear and pink.

PRODUCT
**La Maison du Shogun**
DESIGNER
**Les Maisons de Cartier**
MANUFACTURER
**Cartier**

Created in the purest tradition of French crystal, La Maison du Shogun is a line of stemware, barware and vases in rounded forms, emphasized by dramatic frosted cuts.

PRODUCT
**Stardust Bar Set**
DESIGNER
**David Dowler**
MANUFACTURER
**Steuben**

These glasses and decanter contain air bubbles suggesting a starry sky.

PRODUCT
**Coca-Cola Glass for diet Coca-Cola**
DESIGNER
**William E. Hoffer on behalf of The Coca-Cola Company**
MANUFACTURER
**Durobar S.A., Belgium**
PHOTOGRAPHER
**B.C. Design**

An institutional drinking glass (16 oz., 6⅜″h) for restaurants and soda fountains, this promotional piece is designed with an indented swirl to convey fun, energy, and to give the glass a memorable visual and tactile feature. It won first place in the institutional glassware category of the Society of Glass and Ceramic Decorators annual design competition, 1990.

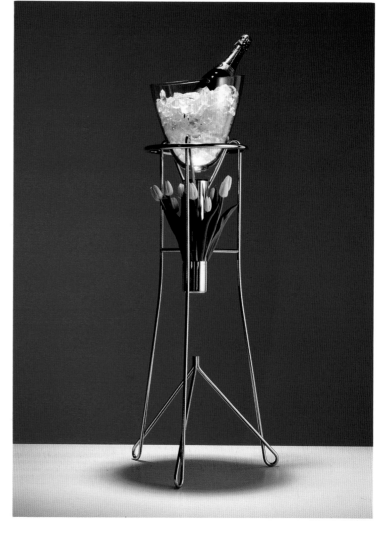

PRODUCT
**Arizona Champagne Valet**
DESIGNER
**Ross Lovegrove**
MANUFACTURER
**Forum, London**
PHOTOGRAPHER
**John Ross**

This dramatic, self-illuminating glass champagne bowl is lighted from below by a heavy duty torch. A gold plated flower vase beneath the cone provides another interesting feature.

PRODUCT
**Lampwork Goblet**
DESIGNER
**John Farrell**
MANUFACTURER
**John Farrell**

In lampworking, glass tubes or rods are heated, bent and worked into various shapes. A lampworked piece must be built up in parts. It can be a long, slow process from conception of the piece to final realization. Once the body of the piece is set, the bowl and base are created by casting molten glass in a mold.

*Available through Mindscape Gallery, Evanston, Illinois.*

PRODUCT
**Gorilla Goblet**
DESIGNERS
**Robert Levin and Ken Carter**
MANUFACTURERS
**Robert Levin and Ken Carter**

All elements of the gorilla goblet are hot worked, the embellishments being formed separately and attached to the hot stem and blown bowl. The gorilla face is formed from hot worked canes of glass and colored fragments and is included in a clear glass stem.

*Available through Mindscape Gallery, Evanston, Illinois.*

PRODUCT
**Fish Goblet**
DESIGNER
**Alan Goldfarb**
MANUFACTURER
**Alan Goldfarb**

Hand blown glass fish goblet. The clear molten glass is rolled into a mound of colored glass chips to produce the brilliant background coloration. Each piece is signed and dated near the tail.

*Available through Mindscape Gallery, Evanston, Illinois.*

PRODUCT
**Ribbon Goblets**
DESIGNER
**Adrienne McStay**
MANUFACTURER
**Adrienne McStay**

Adrienne McStay manipulates glass rods, bending and twisting them to form the stems of her goblets. The hand blown bases and bowls are attached hot to the glass ribbons, the completed piece then going through the annealing cycle.

*Available through Mindscape Gallery, Evanston, Illinois.*

PRODUCT
**Dichroic Goblet**
DESIGNER
**Steven Maslach**
MANUFACTURER
**Steven Maslach**

The Dichroic Goblet series titled "Two Persons Joined" won the grand prize in the 1988 goblet competition, "A Glass For Wine" sponsored by Baccarat Crystal and Taittintger Champagne, as a benefit for the New York Experimental Glass Workshop. This winning design is also in the American Craft Museum's permanent collection.

*Available through Mindscape Gallery, Evanston, Illinois.*

PRODUCT
**Goblets**
DESIGNER
**William Bernstein**
MANUFACTURER
**William Bernstein**

William Bernstein's work is involved with imagery applied to blown forms while they are in a molten state. Images are applied directly on the vessel surface with hot glass canes and with hot applied color fragments of glass.

*Available through Mindscape Gallery, Evanston, Illinois.*

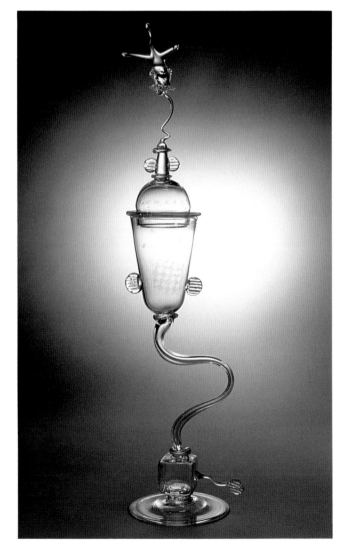

PRODUCT
**"Jack-in-the-box" Goblet**
DESIGNER
**Deborah Czeresko**
MANUFACTURER
**Deborah Czeresko**

Whimsical goblet of hand blown, acid etched glass.

*Available exclusively through Fullscale Design Gallery, New York.*

PRODUCT
**Untitled Goblet**
DESIGNER
**Deborah Czeresko**
MANUFACTURER
**Deborah Czeresko**

Spiral stem goblet of
hand blown and colored
glass.

*Available exclusively through Fullscale
Design Gallery, New York.*

PRODUCT
**"Three-tier Decanter"**
DESIGNER
**Deborah Czeresko**
MANUFACTURER
**Deborah Czeresko**

Hand blown and colored
glass decanter.

*Available exclusively through Fullscale
Design Gallery, New York.*

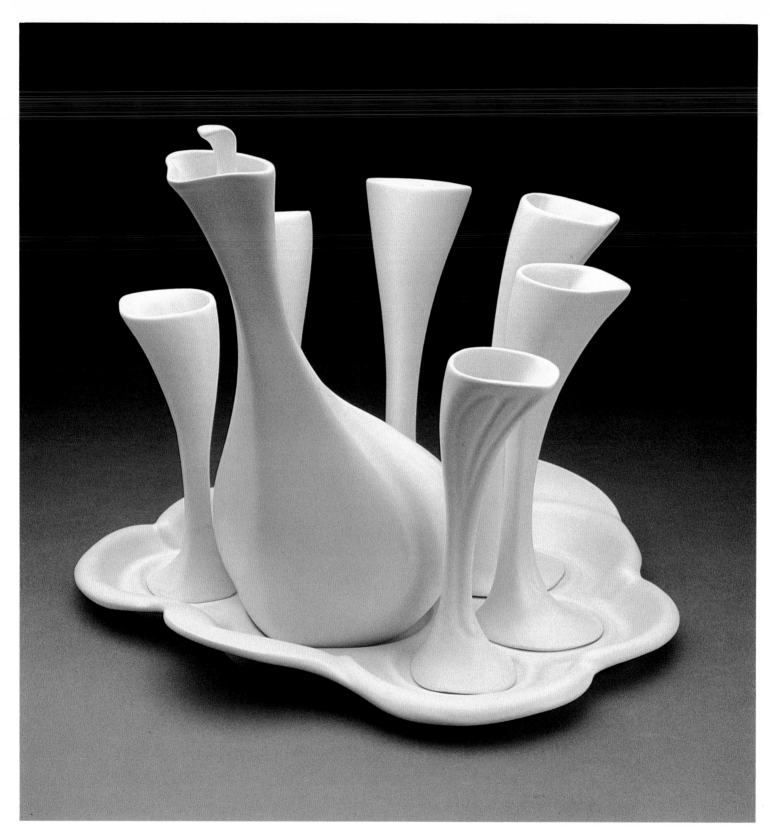

PRODUCT
**Cordial Set**
DESIGNER
**Peter Saenger**
MANUFACTURER
**Saenger Porcelain**
PHOTOGRAPHER
**Alice Sebrill**

Cast porcelain cordial set with a gracefully proportioned decanter (10″h) and six goblets of three different heights (7″, 6″, 5″) placed symmetrically on the accompanying tray.

PRODUCT
**Goblets**
DESIGNER
**Colleen Zufelt-Tomczak**
MANUFACTURER
**Colleen Zufelt-Tomczak**
PHOTOGRAPHER
**Carson Zullinger**

Slip cast, coil and hand-
built goblets in whiteware
with airbrushed under-
glazes.

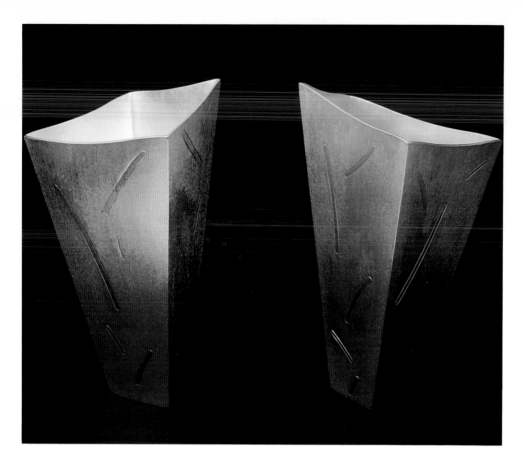

PRODUCT
**Arccups**
DESIGNER
**Cynthia Eid**
MANUFACTURER
**Cynthia Eid**
PHOTOGRAPHER
**Cynthia Eid**

Sterling silver cups with
14 karat gold inlay.

PRODUCT
**Cups**
DESIGNER
**Cynthia Eid**
MANUFACTURER
**Cynthia Eid**
PHOTOGRAPHER
**Cynthia Eid**

Sterling silver cups with
hammered texture.

PRODUCT
**Goblet**
DESIGNER
**Roberta Masur-Maxfield**
MANUFACTURER
**Roberta Masur-Maxfield**
PHOTOGRAPHER
**Jim Ream**

Raised & constructed
brushed sterling silver
goblet with 24 karat
gold plated interior.

PRODUCT
**"Balance II"**
DESIGNER
**Cynthia Eid**
MANUFACTURER
**Cynthia Eid**
PHOTOGRAPHER
**Cynthia Eid**

Pewter goblet.

PRODUCT
**Chalice**
DESIGNER
**William Frederick**
MANUFACTURER
**William Frederick**
PHOTOGRAPHER
**William Frederick**

Sterling silver chalice
with appliqué design.

PRODUCT
**Kiddish Cup**
DESIGNER
**Robyn Nichols**
MANUFACTURER
**Robyn Nichols**
PHOTOGRAPHER
**Hollis Officer**

Willow branch sterling silver kiddish cup with chased leaves. Branches are forged and fabricated.

# CHAPTER FOUR

# Serving Pieces

*Serving pieces in Metaal by Grainware, designed by Michael Lax.*

PRODUCT
**Shell Series**
DESIGNER
**Ann Morhauser**
MANUFACTURER
**Annieglass Studio, Santa Cruz, California**
PHOTOGRAPHER
**Viktor Budnic**

Derived from organic shapes found in nature, these frosted pieces are accented with mottled gold or platinum edges. A limited edition of thicker ⅜″ frosted glass is available in the three largest sizes.

PRODUCT
**Roman Antique Bread Plate**
DESIGNER
**Ann Morhauser**
MANUFACTURER
**Annieglass Studio, Santa Cruz, California**
PHOTOGRAPHER
**Viktor Budnic**

Prior to firing, 24 karat gold is applied freehand to this glass Roman antique bread plate.

PRODUCT
**Slab Series**
DESIGNER
**Ann Morhauser**
MANUFACTURER
**Annieglass Studio, Santa Cruz, California**
PHOTOGRAPHER
**Viktor Budnic**

Sandblasted glass slabs available in a variety of colors and textures: clear; gray faux cement; blue or black with etched Etruscan petroglyphs.

PRODUCT
**Holly Ribbons Oven-to-Tableware**
DESIGNER
**Royal Worcester**
MANUFACTURER
**Royal Worcester**

Fine English Porcelain creates an elegant, practical complement to a formal holiday table.

PRODUCT
**Worcester Herbs Oven-to-Tableware**
DESIGNER
**Royal Worcester**
MANUFACTURER
**Royal Worcester**

Botanical drawings of popular English herbs inspired this porcelain oven-to-tableware. Each piece is freezer, oven, microwave and dishwasher safe.

PRODUCT
**Fairfield Oven-to-Tableware**
DESIGNER
**Royal Worcester**
MANUFACTURER
**Royal Worcester**

Fairfield Oven-to-Table-
ware features bold, fresh
flowers on fine English
porcelain and coordinates
with Fairfield dinnerware.

PRODUCT
**Flora Danica**
DESIGNER
**Royal Copenhagen**
MANUFACTURER
**Royal Copenhagen**

Designed in the 18th century, Flora Danica represents the golden age of porcelain. The many details are modelled and cut out by hand and the flowers are painted on freehand, exactly as they were 200 years ago. (Tureen, covered vegetable dish, round plate with open-work border)

PRODUCT
**Flora Danica Ice Cream Dome
with Dish**
DESIGNER
**Royal Copenhagen**
MANUFACTURER
**Royal Copenhagen**

Details are modelled and
cut out by hand on Royal
Copenhagen's elegant
porcelain ice cream
dome.

(detail)

PRODUCT
**Mesa Serving Pieces**
DESIGNER
**Kathleen Wills**
MANUFACTURER
**Dansk International Designs Ltd.**
High-fired stoneware with a silky glaze, Mesa is oven, dishwasher and microwave safe.

PRODUCT
**Mosaic Completer Set**
DESIGNER
**Victoria Rush Morrison**
MANUFACTURER
**Dansk International Designs Ltd.**

Platter, vegetable bowl, sugar bowl and creamer in the Tile motif complements patterns in Dansk's Mosaic Collection.

PRODUCT
**Salad or Pasta Bowl**
DESIGNER
**Wesley Dunn**
MANUFACTURER
**Wesley Dunn**
PHOTOGRAPHER
**Wesley Dunn**

Multi-use hand thrown ceramic bowl in vivid periwinkle and white sealed with a gloss glaze.

PRODUCT
**Fish Bowls**
DESIGNER
**Wesley Dunn**
MANUFACTURER
**Wesley Dunn**
PHOTOGRAPHER
**Wesley Dunn**

Decorative and functional hand thrown ceramic bowls with underwater motif featuring fish, coral and marine plants on a background of black dots. Two from a series of ten.

PRODUCT
**Bowl with Black and White Apples**
DESIGNERS
**Teraki/Bisson**
**Romulus Craft**
MANUFACTURER
**Teraki/Bisson**
**Romulus Craft**
PHOTOGRAPHER
**Romulus Craft**

This thrown porcelain bowl features contrast in texture and color, with a lustrous white, clear glazed exterior and black oxide interior.

PRODUCT
**Fruit Tray**
DESIGNER
**Marek Cecula**
MANUFACTURER
**Marek Cecula/Contemporary Porcelain**
PHOTOGRAPHER
**Bill Waltzer**

Ideal for serving fruit or appetizers, this porcelain tray has a matte finish that enhances the glazed indentations. Available in slate or white.

PRODUCT
**"Disc Form"**
DESIGNER
**Marek Cecula**
MANUFACTURER
**Marek Cecula/Contemporary Porcelain**
PHOTOGRAPHER
**Bill Waltzer**

Multi-use round serving form in blue-gray porcelain with black glaze.

PRODUCT
**Creamer and Sugar**
DESIGNER
**Marek Cecula**
MANUFACTURER
**Marek Cecula/Contemporary Porcelain**
PHOTOGRAPHER
**Yoshiko Ebihara**

A positive/negative concept forms the basis of the geometric design for this porcelain sugar and creamer. Each element has rubber feet to prevent slipping.

*Available through Gallery 91, New York.*

PRODUCT
**"Square Form"**
DESIGNER
**Marek Cecula**
MANUFACTURER
**Marek Cecula/Contemporary Porcelain**
PHOTOGRAPHER
**Bill Waltzer**

Multi-use blue-gray, square, porcelain serving form with black glaze.

PRODUCT
**Sugar and Creamer**
DESIGNER
**Peter Saenger**
MANUFACTURER
**Saenger Porcelain**
PHOTOGRAPHER
**Alice Sebrill**

Opaque glazed cast porcelain sugar and creamer with tray.

PRODUCT
**Sugar and Creamer**
DESIGNER
**Peter Saenger**
MANUFACTURER
**Saenger Porcelain**
PHOTOGRAPHER
**Alice Sebrill**

Pleasing to the eye and hand, this harmoniously designed cast porcelain sugar and creamer has a glossy opaque glazed interior and matte exterior.

PRODUCT
**Pitcher with Cups**
DESIGNER
**Marek Cecula**
MANUFACTURER
**Marek Cecula**
PHOTOGRAPHER
**Bill Waltzer**

Hand crafted porcelain
pitcher with cups in yel-
low, apple green and
cobalt.

PRODUCT
**Pitcher and Cup**
DESIGNER
**Marek Cecula**
MANUFACTURER
**Marek Cecula/Contemporary
Porcelain**
PHOTOGRAPHER
**Bill Waltzer**

Double-handle pitcher
for cold drinks
shown with one cup
in a set of four. Blue-gray
porcelain with black
glazed interior.

PRODUCT
**Water Jug**
DESIGNER
**Randy Stromsoe**
MANUFACTURER
**Randy Stromsoe**
PHOTOGRAPHERS
**Ron and Frank Bez**

Handmade, polished
pewter water jug, also
available in sterling silver.

PRODUCT
**Pitchers**
DESIGNER
**Randy Stromsoe**
MANUFACTURER
**Randy Stromsoe, Stromsoe
Studios**
PHOTOGRAPHERS
**Ron and Frank Bez**

Creamers in varying sizes
in dark patina pewter.

PRODUCT
**Dancing Shakers/Salt and Pepper**
DESIGNER
**Sue L. Amendolara**
MANUFACTURER
**Sue L. Amendolara**
PHOTOGRAPHER
**Rick Potteiger**

Whimsical "dancing" salt and pepper shakers in sterling silver, ebony, 24 karat gold foil and mother-of-pearl. (Salt: $4'' \times 5'' \times 1\frac{1}{2}''$) The reversed placement of materials in each piece intensifies the shakers' playfulness.

PRODUCT
**Salt and Pepper**
DESIGNER
**Robyn Nichols**
MANUFACTURER
**Robyn Nichols**
PHOTOGRAPHER
**Hollis Officer**

Garlic top hand formed sterling silver salt and pepper shakers.

PRODUCT
**Olive Oil Container**
DESIGNER
**Curtis K. LaFollette**
MANUFACTURER
**Curtis K. LaFollette**
PHOTOGRAPHER
**Nash Studio**

Finely finished sterling
silver olive oil container
with tapered pouring
spout on a brass
platform.

PRODUCT
**Spreader and Server**
DESIGNER
**Michael Lax**
MANUFACTURER
**The Grainware Company**

An elegant way to present butter, paté or soft cheese, this spreader and server are cast in a specially-formulated metal alloy.

*Designed exclusively for Grainware by Michael Lax.*

PRODUCT
**Pair of Serving Dishes**
DESIGNER
**William Frederick**
PHOTOGRAPHER
**William Frederick**

Cast sterling silver serving dishes.

PRODUCT
**METAAL™ Signature Bowl**
DESIGNER
**Michael Lax**
MANUFACTURER
**The Grainware Company**

Both functional and
appealing, the Sig-
nature Bowl is avail-
able in three sizes.

*Designed exclusively for Grainware by
Michael Lax.*

PRODUCT
**Oval Bowl**
DESIGNER
**Michael Lax**
MANUFACTURER
**The Grainware Company**

Sculpture in motion, this oval bowl cast in a specially-formulated metal alloy (METAAL™) can also stand alone as a decorative accessory.

*Designed exclusively for Grainware by Michael Lax.*

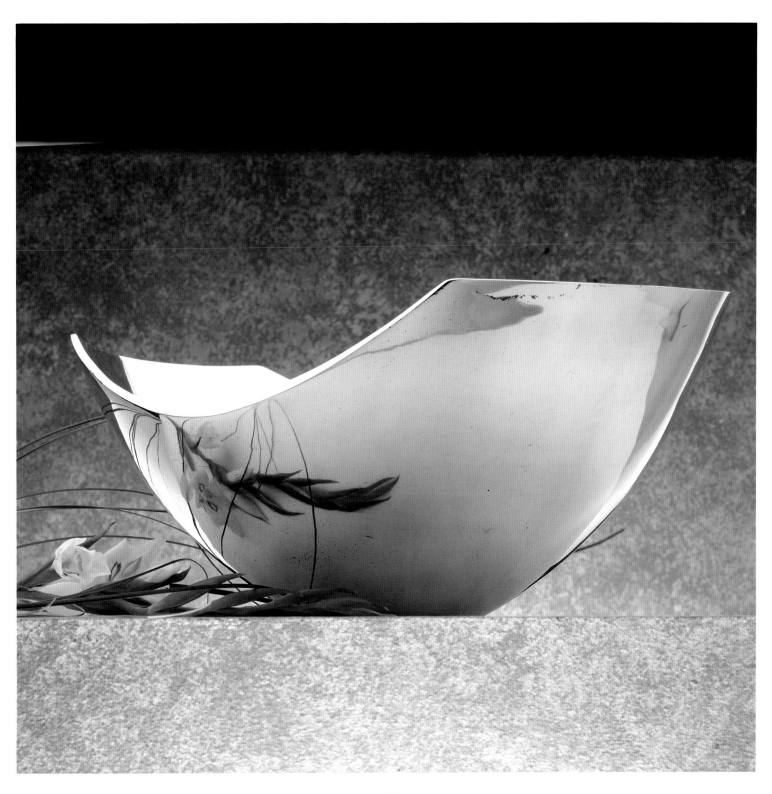

PRODUCT
**METAAL™ Divided Vegetable Bowl**
DESIGNER
**Michael Lax**
MANUFACTURER
**The Grainware Company**

Excellent heat retention
is an outstanding feature
of the METAAL™ di-
vided vegetable bowl.

*Designed exclusively for Grainware by
Michael Lax.*

PRODUCT
**METAAL**™ **Pebble Server**
DESIGNER
**Michael Lax**
MANUFACTURER
**The Grainware Company**

Winner of the International Tabletop Competition for design excellence, this piece is generously proportioned and unusually shaped.

*Designed exclusively for Grainware by Michael Lax.*

# CHAPTER FIVE

# Coffee and Tea Services

*Tea service in Warmstry White Fine Bone China, designed and manufactured by Royal Worcester.*

PRODUCT
**Tea Service**
MANUFACTURER
**Stangl Pottery, USA**

Glazed ceramic tea service, c. 1928–1929.

*The Mitchell Wolfson, Jr. Collection
Courtesy The Wolfsonian Foundation
Miami, Florida*

PRODUCT
**Tea Service**
MANUFACTURER
**Belleek Pottery**

Glazed porcelain Fan Tea Ware tea service, c. 1921.

*The Mitchell Wolfson, Jr. Collection
Courtesy The Wolfsonian Foundation
Miami, Florida*

PRODUCT
**Coffee and Tea Service**
DESIGNER
**Kem** *(attributed to Weber)*
MANUFACTURER
**Porter Blanchard Co.**

Silver, ivory and bakelite
coffee and tea service,
c. 1935–1940.

*The Mitchell Wolfson, Jr. Collection*
*Courtesy The Wolfsonian Foundation*
*Miami, Florida*

PRODUCT
**Tea Service**
DESIGNER
**Unknown, India**

Footed silver tea service
with plastic handles and
finials, c. 1920–1925.

*The Mitchell Wolfson, Jr. Collection*
*Courtesy The Wolfsonian Foundation*
*Miami, Florida*

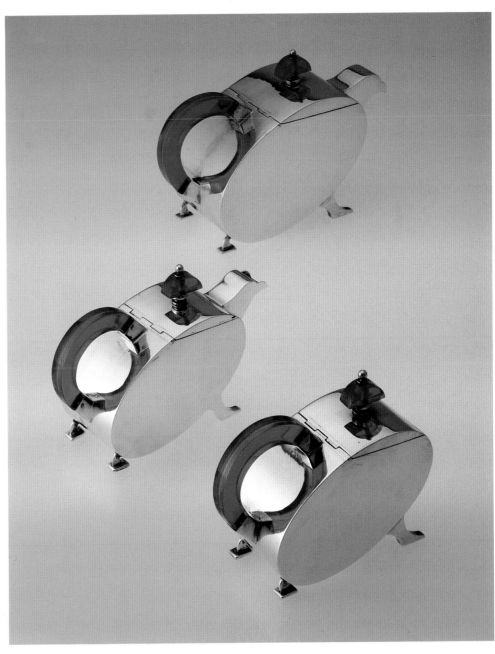

PRODUCT
**Coffee Service**
DESIGNER
**Josef Hoffmann, Austria**

Gilded porcelain coffee
service, 1930.

*The Mitchell Wolfson, Jr. Collection*
*Courtesy The Wolfsonian Foundation*
*Miami, Florida*

PRODUCT
**Tea Service**
DESIGNER
**Narotamdas Bhau, India**

Silver, celluloid tea service with gazelle motif,
c. 1920–1929.

*The Mitchell Wolfson, Jr. Collection*
*Courtesy The Wolfsonian Foundation*
*Miami, Florida*

PRODUCT
**Gropius Tea Service**
DESIGNER
**Walter Gropius**
MANUFACTURER
**Rosenthal, Germany**

This tea set offers a perfect harmony of form and function. While pouring, the teapot and its lid can be held with one hand. Cups and plates are of pure white porcelain, while the teapot, sugar, creamer and saucers are made of Porcelain Noire, the world's only black porcelain.

*Available through Rosenthal Design Showroom, Dania, Florida*

PRODUCT
**Blue Colonel Fine Bone China**
DESIGNER
**Spode**
MANUFACTURER
**Spode**

Designed in the fluted Chelsea shape, Blue Colonel is based on a Chinese design from the 15th century.

PRODUCT
**Trapnell Sprays Fine Bone China**
DESIGNER
**Spode**
MANUFACTURER
**Spode**

Designed in the fluted Chelsea shape, Trapnell Sprays has an exquisite double gold band and turquoise border.

PRODUCT
**"Corolla"**
DESIGNER
**Villeroy & Boch**
MANUFACTURER
**Villeroy & Boch**

A china coffee service, "Corolla" features graphic blooms in vibrant shades of pink, orange and lilac. The "rechaud" pot warmer and bread board-like individual tray are reflective of its European origins.

PRODUCT
**SWANN**
DESIGNER
**Borek Sipek**
MANUFACTURER
**Driade**

White porcelain teapot with benjaron decoration and silver plated parts.

*Available through Stilnovo, Coral Gables, Florida*

PRODUCT
**Tea Set**
DESIGNER
**Colleen Zufelt-Tomczak**
MANUFACTURER
**Colleen Zufelt-Tomczak**
PHOTOGRAPHER
**Carson Zullinger**

This decorative, pastel tea set includes a wheel-thrown teapot, four slip cast and hand-built teacups, and a slab tray, all with airbrushed underglazes.

PRODUCT
**Teapots**
DESIGNERS
**Teraki/Bisson**
**Romulus Craft**
MANUFACTURER
**Teraki/Bisson**
**Romulus Craft**
PHOTOGRAPHER
**Romulus Craft**

Black and white porcelain teapots on porcelain pedestals.

PRODUCT
**Tea or Coffee Set**
DESIGNER
**Marek Cecula**
MANUFACTURER
**Marek Cecula/Contemporary Porcelain**

Color coordinated in apple green and cobalt, this hand crafted porcelain set is appropriate for either tea or coffee.

PRODUCT
**Tea Set**
DESIGNER
**Peter Saenger**
MANUFACTURER
**Saenger Porcelain**
PHOTOGRAPHER
**Alice Sebrill**

Cast porcelain teapot with four 8-ounce cups and tray, designed to provide both utility and sculpture. Dishwasher and microwave safe.

PRODUCT
**Ceremonial Set I**
DESIGNER
**Marek Cecula**
MANUFACTURER
**Marek Cecula/Contemporary Porcelain**
PHOTOGRAPHER
**Yoshiko Ebihara**

Tea service or saki set handmade in porcelain. The triangular tray serves as a pedestal and is indented in three places to accept the pot and cups.

*Available through Gallery 91, New York.*

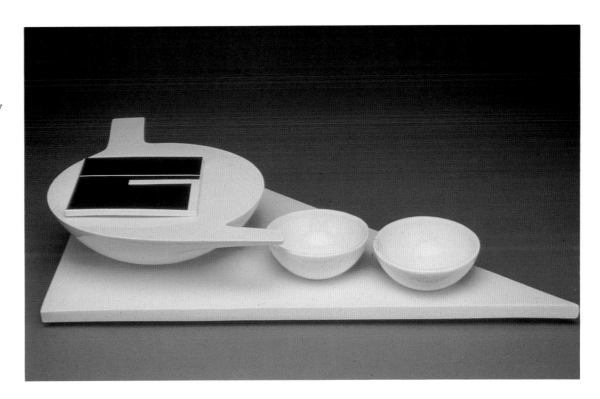

PRODUCT
**Ceremonial Set II**
DESIGNER
**Marek Cecula**
MANUFACTURER
**Marek Cecula/Contemporary Porcelain**
PHOTOGRAPHER
**Bill Waltzer**

A distinctive feature of this porcelain tea service/saki set is the built-in positive/negative fit between the tray and the elements: a relief on the tray is accommodated by indentations on the bottom of the cups and pot.

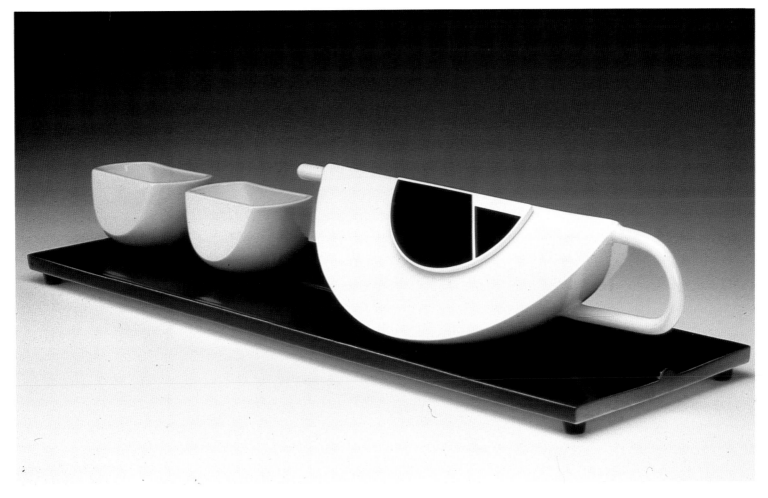

PRODUCT
**"Lovers Set" Saki or
Demitasse Set**
DESIGNER
**Marek Cecula**
MANUFACTURER
**Marek Cecula/Contemporary
Porcelain**
PHOTOGRAPHER
**Bill Waltzer**

Translucent slip cast porcelain saki/demitasse set (7"h) on black glazed tray. Contrasting handles are metal with colorful plastic accents.

PRODUCT
**"Future Form"**
DESIGNER
**Marek Cecula**
MANUFACTURER
**Marek Cecula/Contemporary
Porcelain**
PHOTOGRAPHER
**Bill Waltzer**

The "Future Form" teapot (6½"h), shown with one cup in a set of four, is slip cast, glazed porcelain with a red overglaze.

PRODUCT
**Teapot**
DESIGNER
**Curtis K. LaFollette**
MANUFACTURER
**Curtis K. LaFollette**
PHOTOGRAPHER
**Nash Studio**

A painted red masonite handle and finial accent this hand raised and fabricated copper teapot. It holds approximately 20 ounces.

PRODUCT
**"So You Only Wanted Half a Cup?"**
DESIGNER
**Curtis K. LaFollette**
MANUFACTURER
**Curtis K. LaFollette**
PHOTOGRAPHER
**Nash Studio**

A whimsical visual statement, this hand-raised and fabricated copper teapot has a silver plated interior and American walnut handle.

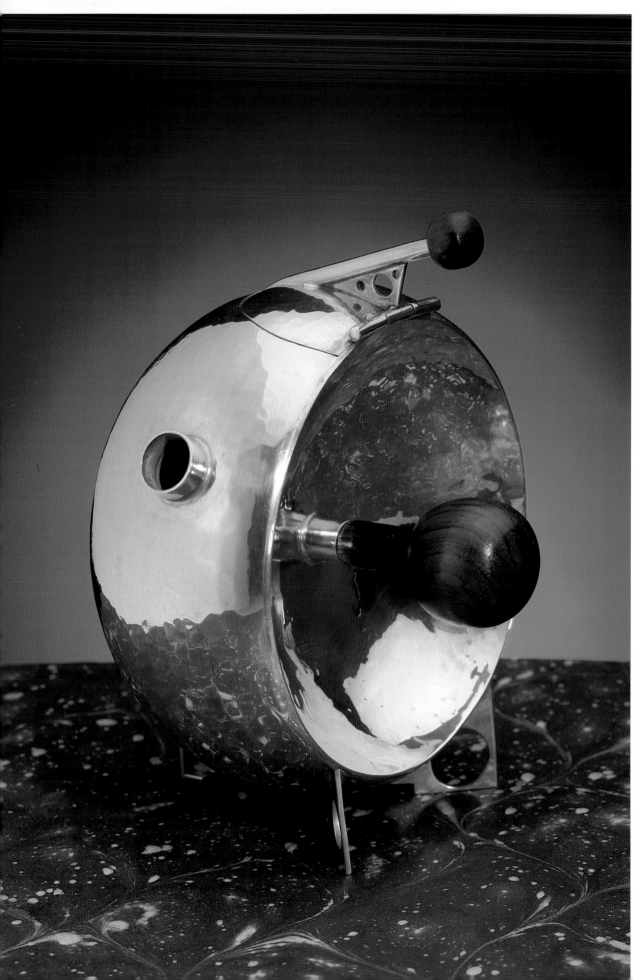

PRODUCT
**Teapot**
DESIGNER
**Curtis K. LaFollette**
MANUFACTURER
**Curtis K. LaFollette**
PHOTOGRAPHER
**Nash Studio**

Copper and inlaid sterling silver teapot utilizing a 17th-century Japanese process. The rosewood finial and handle are lathe-turned.

PRODUCT
**Coffee Server**
DESIGNER
**Curtis K. LaFollette**
MANUFACTURER
**Curtis K. LaFollette**
PHOTOGRAPHER
**Nash Studio**

Fabricated copper coffee server with lathe-turned walnut handle.

PRODUCT
**Teapot**
DESIGNER
**Curtis K. LaFollette**
PHOTOGRAPHER
**Nash Studio**

Uniquely shaped, hand-raised and fabricated copper teapot with silver plated interior and fine-grained walnut handle.

PRODUCT
**Teapot**
DESIGNER
**Curtis K. LaFollette**
MANUFACTURER
**Curtis K. LaFollette**
PHOTOGRAPHER
**Nash Studio**

This elegant, finely finished, hammered copper teapot is topped by distinctive purple heartwood set in a sterling silver lid.

PRODUCT
**Teapot**
DESIGNER
**Curtis K. LaFollette**
MANUFACTURER
**Curtis K. LaFollette**
PHOTOGRAPHER
**Nash Studio**

The carved masonite finial and handle distinguish this beautifully shaped, hammered teapot.

PRODUCT
**Bulls–eye Teapot**
DESIGNER
**Susan Ewing**
**INTERALIA/Design**
MANUFACTURER
**Susan Ewing**
**INTERALIA/Design**
PHOTOGRAPHER
**Rick Potteiger**

This whimsical teapot combines sterling silver with 24 karat vermeil.

PRODUCT
**Penetrated Sphere Teapot**
DESIGNER
**Susan Ewing**
**INTERALIA/Design**
MANUFACTURER
**Susan Ewing**
**INTERALIA/Design**
PHOTOGRAPHER
**Rick Potteiger**

Sterling silver teapot.

PRODUCT
**OBOR 1 Coffee Server**
DESIGNER
**Susan Ewing**
**INTERALIA/Design**
MANUFACTURER
**Susan Ewing**
**INTERALIA/Design**
PHOTOGRAPHER
**Rick Potteiger**

Cylindrical coffee server with distinctive band motif in 24 karat gold plate.

PRODUCT
**OBOR 2 Coffee Server**
DESIGNER
**Susan Ewing**
**INTERALIA/Design**
MANUFACTURER
**Susan Ewing**
**INTERALIA/Design**
PHOTOGRAPHER
**Rick Potteiger**

Coffee server in 24 karat gold plate with a distinctive purple heartwood handle.

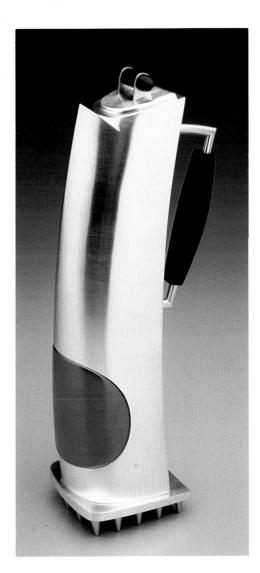

PRODUCT
**Cycladic Figure Impregnated**
DESIGNER
**Thomas P. Muir**
MANUFACTURER
**Thomas P. Muir**
PHOTOGRAPHER
**Rob Wheless**

Coffee server in sterling silver, 18 karat gold and oxidized copper (red), with anodized aluminum handle (black). Formed and fabricated.

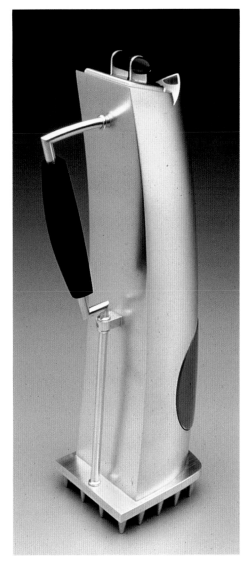

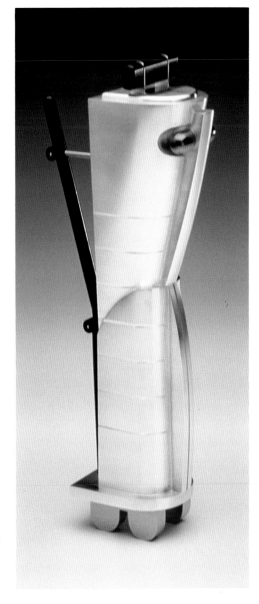

PRODUCT
**Earth Mother**
DESIGNER
**Thomas P. Muir**
MANUFACTURER
**Thomas P. Muir**
PHOTOGRAPHER
**Rob Wheless**

Espresso server in sterling silver, 18 karat gold and oxidized copper (red), with anodized aluminum handle (black).

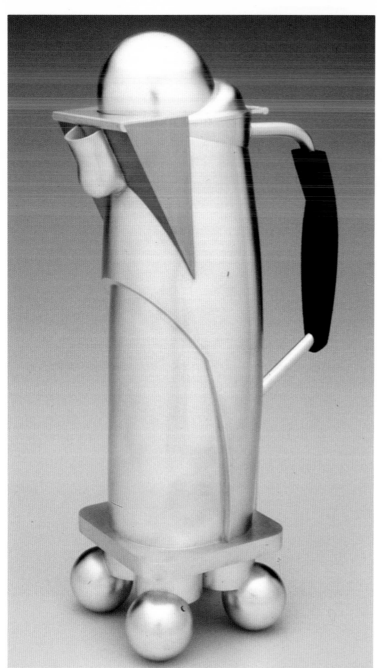

PRODUCT
**Beluga Espresso Server**
DESIGNER
**Thomas P. Muir**
MANUFACTURER
**Thomas P. Muir**
PHOTOGRAPHER
**Thomas P. Muir**

Sterling silver and nickel espresso coffee server with oxidized and anodized aluminum handle. Formed, cast, fabricated.

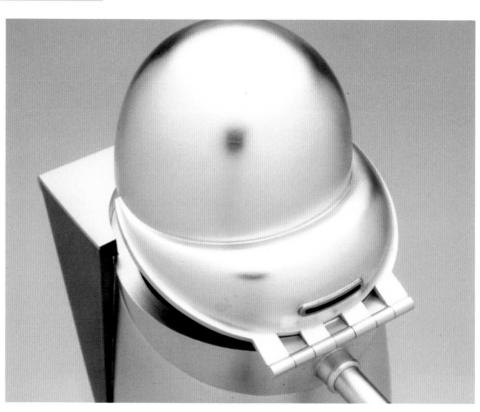

PRODUCT
**Teapot**
DESIGNER
**William Frederick**
MANUFACTURER
**William Frederick**
PHOTOGRAPHER
**William Frederick**

Sterling silver teapot.

PRODUCT
**Silver Service**
DESIGNER
**Thomas R. Markusen**
MANUFACTURER
**Thomas R. Markusen**
PHOTOGRAPHER
**Jim Dusen**

Sterling silver coffee service with Delrin handles.

PRODUCT
**Winged Pitcher and Sugar,**
**Camouflaged**
DESIGNER
**Susan Ewing**
**INTERALIA/Design**
MANUFACTURER
**Susan Ewing**
**INTERALIA/Design**
PHOTOGRAPHER
**Rick Potteiger**

Pitcher and sugar with
camouflage pattern in
sterling silver and 24
karat vermeil.

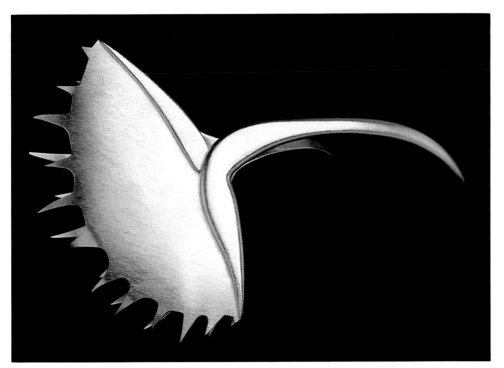

PRODUCT
**Flytrap Tea Infuser**
DESIGNER
**Sue L. Amendolara**
MANUFACTURER
**Sue L. Amendolara**
PHOTOGRAPHER
**Jeff Sabo**

Sterling silver tea infuser
(7″ × 4½″ × 3″) inspired by
the Venus flytrap and
made using traditional
silversmithing methods.
A spring holds the in-
fuser closed while at rest.
Slots at the top allow the
tea to steep.

PRODUCT
**Miniature Tea Service**
DESIGNERS
**Michael and Maureen Banner**
MANUFACTURER
**Michael and Maureen Banner**
PHOTOGRAPHER
**Paul J. Rocheleau**

Sterling silver miniature
tea service and tray.

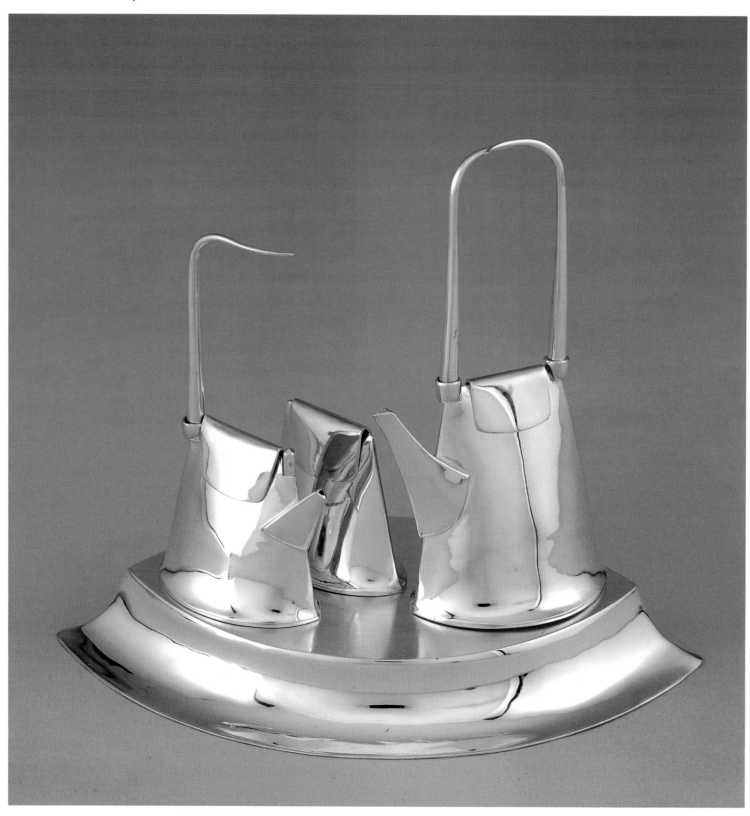

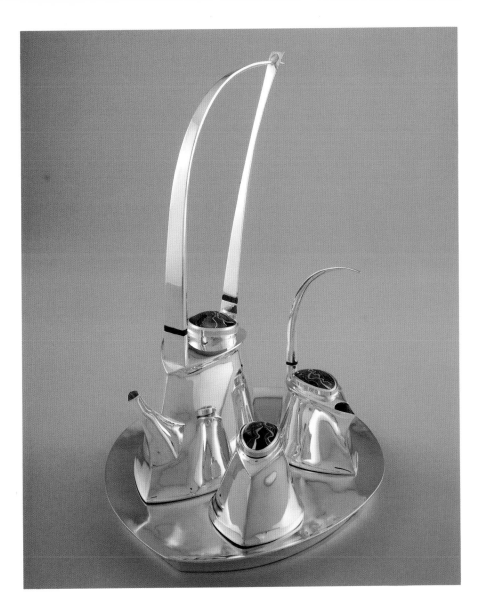

PRODUCT
**Tea Service**
DESIGNERS
**Michael and Maureen Banner**
MANUFACTURER
**Michael and Maureen Banner**
PHOTOGRAPHER
**Paul J. Rocheleau**

Sterling silver tea
service with cloissoné
(on fine silver) lids.

PRODUCT
**Teapot**
DESIGNERS
**Michael and Maureen Banner**
MANUFACTURER
**Michael and Maureen Banner**
PHOTOGRAPHER
**Paul J. Rocheleau**

Sterling silver teapot
with cloissoné lid and
rosewood handle spacers.

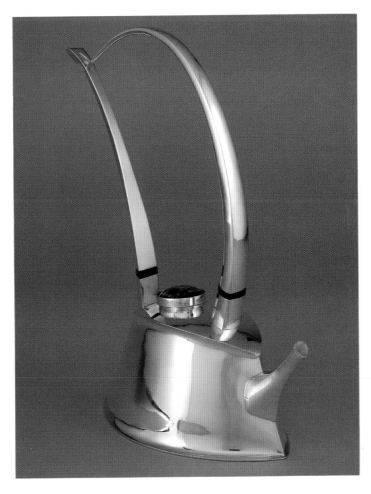

PRODUCT
**Star Teapot**
DESIGNER
**Randy Stromsoe**
MANUFACTURER
**Randy Stromsoe, Stromsoe Studios**
PHOTOGRAPHERS
**Ron and Frank Bez**

Teapot with star motif in dark patina pewter, polished pewter, 23 karat gold leaf and glass.

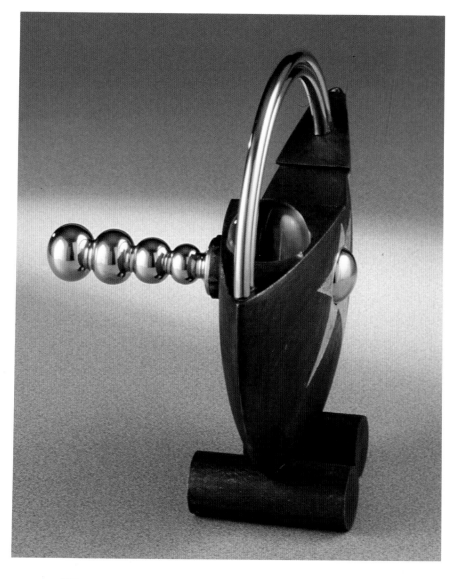

PRODUCT
**Coffee Service, Cup, Spoon**
DESIGNER
**Roberta Masur-Maxfield**
MANUFACTURER
**Roberta Masur-Maxfield**
PHOTOGRAPHER
**Jim Ream**

Raised and constructed
sterling silver coffee service with hand-carved
rosewood handles. The
sterling silver cup has a
gold plated interior.

# CHAPTER SIX

# Table Accessories

*Tablescape, with hand-carved teakwood Koi fish centerpiece, designed by Al Evans, Al Evans Interiors, Inc.*

*Photo: Dan Forer*

PRODUCT
**Equipoise**
DESIGNER
**Cynthia Eid**
MANUFACTURER
**Cynthia Eid**
PHOTOGRAPHER
**Cynthia Eid**

Sterling silver vase.

PRODUCT
**Sterling Compote**
DESIGNER
**Harold Rogovin**
MANUFACTURER
**Harold Rogovin**
PHOTOGRAPHER
**Elton Pope-Lance**

Hammered sterling silver compote with cast leaves.

PRODUCT
**Odette**
DESIGNER
**Borek Sipek**
MANUFACTURER
**Driade**

White porcelain fruit
dish with blue decoration
and silver plated base.

*Available through Stilnovo, Coral Gables,
Florida*

PRODUCT
**Obelisk Vases**
DESIGNER
**Marek Cecula**
MANUFACTURER
**Marek Cecula/Contemporary
Porcelain**
PHOTOGRAPHER
**Bill Waltzer**

Lyrical interactive vases
in porcelain with a matte
finish.

PRODUCT
**Flower Vases**
DESIGNER
**William Frederick**
MANUFACTURER
**William Frederick**
PHOTOGRAPHER
**Arling Studio**

Hand formed sterling sil-
ver flower vases.

PRODUCT
**Column Bowl**
DESIGNER
**Randy Stromsoe**
MANUFACTURER
**Randy Stromsoe, Stromsoe Studios**
PHOTOGRAPHERS
**Ron and Frank Bez**

Polished pewter column bowl, also available in sterling.

PRODUCT
**Bowl with Stand**
DESIGNER
**Randy Stromsoe**
MANUFACTURER
**Randy Stromsoe, Stromsoe Studios**
PHOTOGRAPHERS
**Ron and Frank Bez**

Sterling silver bowl with three-leg stand.

PRODUCT
**Centerpiece**
DESIGNER
**Randy Stromsoe**
MANUFACTURER
**Randy Stromsoe, Stromsoe Studios**
PHOTOGRAPHERS
**Ron and Frank Bez**

Elegant centerpiece in polished pewter.

PRODUCT
**Centerpiece**
DESIGNER
**Randy Stromsoe**
MANUFACTURER
**Randy Stromsoe, Stromsoe Studios**
PHOTOGRAPHERS
**Ron and Frank Bez**

The contrast between sterling silver and dark pewter enhances this handsome centerpiece.

PRODUCT
**Torch Bowl**
DESIGNER
**Randy Stromsoe**
MANUFACTURER
**Randy Stromsoe, Stromsoe Studios**
PHOTOGRAPHERS
**Ron and Frank Bez**

Sterling silver bowl with a distinctive dark pewter base.

PRODUCT
**Bowl and Pedestal IV**
DESIGNER
**Ann E. Grigsby**
MANUFACTURER
**Ann E. Grigsby**
PHOTOGRAPHER
**Devery Weeks**

Shimmering surfaces and sculptural forms express grace and elegance in this outstanding centerpiece. The bowl is spun, sterling silver with a satin finish.

PRODUCT
**Bowl and Pedestal V**
DESIGNER
**Ann E. Grigsby**
MANUFACTURER
**Ann E. Grigsby**
PHOTOGRAPHER
**Devery Weeks**

Glass and sterling are effectively combined in this gleaming centerpiece. The bowl is fabricated sterling silver with satin finish.

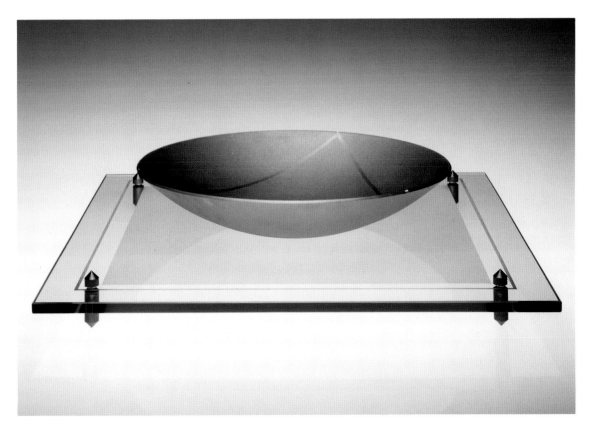

PRODUCT
**Bowl and Pedestal I**
DESIGNER
**Ann E. Grigsby**
MANUFACTURER
**Ann E. Grigsby**
PHOTOGRAPHER
**Devery Weeks**

This elegant piece can be used as a table or buffet centerpiece. The bowl is spun, anodized aluminum with a sandblasted finish.

PRODUCT
**Bowl and Pedestal III**
DESIGNER
**Ann E. Grigsby**
MANUFACTURER
**Ann E. Grigsby**
PHOTOGRAPHER
**Devery Weeks**

A spun, anodized aluminum bowl and glass tray create a dynamic centerpiece.

PRODUCT
**Suijin**
DESIGNER
**Yonosuke Iwai**
MANUFACTURER
**ELISO**
PHOTOGRAPHER
**Yoshiko Ebihara**

Cast bronze flower vase with gold interior, silver detail and Urushi patina finish.

*Available through Gallery 91, New York.*

PRODUCT
**Con Crete**
DESIGNER
**Emanuela Frattini**
MANUFACTURER
**EFM New York, Milan**

Candlesticks, base in resin reinforced plaster with polished aluminum candle holders.

PRODUCT
**Footed Gold Slab**
DESIGNER
**Ann Morhauser**
MANUFACTURER
**Annieglass Studio, Santa Cruz, California**
PHOTOGRAPHER
**Viktor Budnic**

Slumped and gilded ½″ glass slab designed for multiple uses.

PRODUCT
**Starlight Cluster**
DESIGNER
**David Dowler**
MANUFACTURER
**Steuben**

Each member of this romantic candlestick trio combines geometric elements of clear and bubbled crystal in varying sequences.

PRODUCT
**Menorah**
DESIGNER
**Robyn Nichols**
MANUFACTURER
**Robyn Nichols**
PHOTOGRAPHER
**Hollis Officer**

Willow branch menorah of hand formed sterling silver wire with fabricated holders.

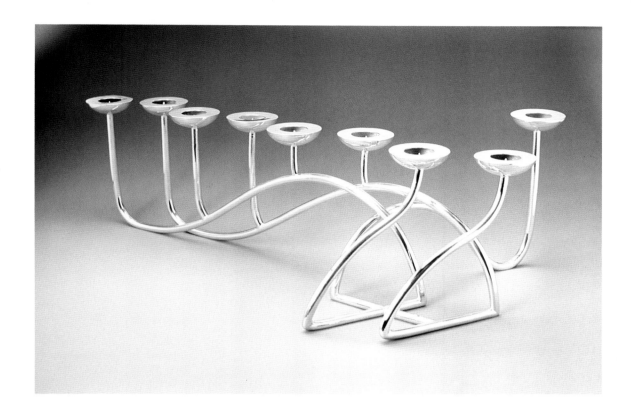

PRODUCT
**Cartier Lapis Collection**
DESIGNER
**Les Maisons de Cartier**
MANUFACTURER
**Cartier**

The striking contrast of lapis lazuli semi-precious stones, beautifully set in silverplate, distinguishes the new Cartier Lapis Collection of giftware that includes a bud vase, picture frame, candlesticks, Champagne bucket, ice bucket, bottle coaster, paperweight and salt and pepper shakers.

PRODUCT
**"Lightning" Candlestick,
"Sun" Candlestick**
DESIGNER
**Bob Gereke**
MANUFACTURER
**Bob Gereke**

Thrown and hand built
porcelain candlesticks
with a high fire glaze.

PRODUCT
**Untitled Candle Holders and
Frame**
DESIGNER
**Ashka Dymel**
MANUFACTURER
**Ashka Dymel**

Polished slate and color-core candle holders and picture frame.

*Available exclusively through Fullscale Design Gallery, New York.*

PRODUCT
**Kaori Incense Burners and
Akari Candle Stand**
DESIGNER
**Ryuya Aoki**
MANUFACTURER
**ELISO**
PHOTOGRAPHER
**Yoshiko Ebihara**

Incense burners and candle stand of lacquered wood with bronze, gold and rodium patina.

*Available through Gallery 91, New York.*

PRODUCT
**Fujin**
DESIGNER
**Yonosuke Iwai**
MANUFACTURER
**ELISO**
PHOTOGRAPHER
**Yoshiko Ebihara**

Cast bronze incense burner accented with silver arms and a gold lid.

*Available through Gallery 91, New York.*

PRODUCT
**Menorah**
DESIGNER
**Harold Rogovin**
MANUFACTURER
**Harold Rogovin**
PHOTOGRAPHER
**Elton Pope-Lance**

Graceful lines distinguish
this sterling silver menorah with a repeated oak
leaf and acorn motif.

PRODUCT
**Nickel Holloware**
DESIGNER
**Thomas R. Markusen**
MANUFACTURER
**Thomas R. Markusen**
PHOTOGRAPHER
**Joe A. Watson**

Handmade by a hot
forming process, these
accessories are copper
with electroplated nickel
finish. The clock has blue
enamel detailing and a
brass face.

PRODUCT
**"Bulls-eye" Candle Holder and "Tummer" Bowls**
DESIGNERS
**Guido Rodriguez, Emmanuel Alouche**
MANUFACTURERS
**Guido Rodriguez, Emmanuel Alouche**

Polished aluminum candle holder with rubber grommet designed by Guido Rodriguez. Polished and sandblasted stainless steel bowls by Emmanuel Alouche.

*Available exclusively through Fullscale Design Gallery, New York.*

PRODUCT
**Copper Holloware**
DESIGNER
**Thomas R. Markusen**
MANUFACTURER
**Thomas R. Markusen**
PHOTOGRAPHER
**Joe A. Watson**

This copper holloware is handmade by a hot forming process and has a beautiful, heat-oxidized patina that is protected against fingerprints by an acrylic epoxy spray.

PRODUCT
**MARCEL**
DESIGNER
**Borek Sipek**
MANUFACTURER
**Driade**

Colorless and blue Bo-
hemia crystal candle
holder with gold plated
metal.

*Available through Stilnovo, Coral Gables,
Florida*

PRODUCT
**Candle Snuffer**
DESIGNER
**Henry Petzal**
MANUFACTURER
**Henry Petzal**

The lotus leaf motif on
the handle of this sterling
silver candle snuffer was
designed to match a pair
of candlesticks, each with
24 lotus leaves.

PRODUCT
**Candle Holders**
DESIGNER
**Ronald Hayes Pearson**
MANUFACTURER
**Ronald Hayes Pearson**
PHOTOGRAPHER
**William Thuss** © 1990 **All rights reserved**

Pair of forged sterling silver candle holders.

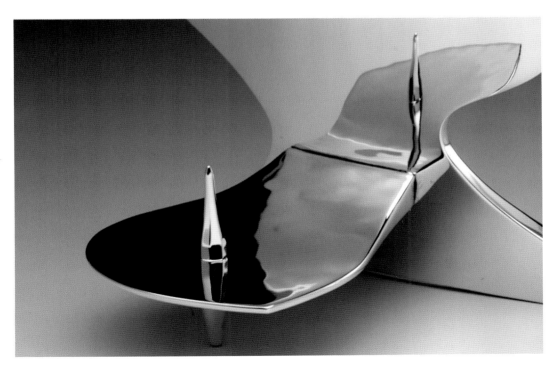

(detail)

# Vases

PRODUCT
**Nimassi Bowl, Tolikan Vase**
DESIGNER
**Joel Smith**
MANUFACTURER
**Steuben**

Named for the Navajo word meaning "round one," the Nimassi Bowl echoes southwestern Native American pottery shapes.

A blown vase, "Tolikan" is the Navajo word for "sweet water," a reference to the life-sustaining contents for which the Native American vessels are intended.

PRODUCT
**Hellenic Urn**
DESIGNER
**Robert Cassetti**
MANUFACTURER
**Steuben**

Blown vase with heavy base incorporates both the dignity of ancient Greek vessels and a classic Steuben design signature, the curled "bit."

PRODUCT
**Empire Vase**
DESIGNER
**Joel Smith**
MANUFACTURER
**Steuben**

Classic blown form reflecting a style popular during Napoleon's reign in France. It's simplicity belies the complex glassmaking techniques used to recreate this eighteenth-century elegance.

PRODUCT
**Archaic Vessels**
DESIGNER
**Michael Graves**
MANUFACTURER
**Steuben**

Archaic vases and bowl in
glass, inspired by Etrus-
can forms.

PRODUCT
**Crystal Peaches and Bouquet**
**Vase**
DESIGNERS
**David Dowler**
**George Thompson**
MANUFACTURER
**Steuben**

Solid crystal peaches capture the delectable qual-
ity of perfectly ripened
fruit. The narrow waist
of George Thompson's
Bouquet Vase gives snug
support to single stems
or small floral arrange-
ment.

PRODUCT
**Cupola**
DESIGNERS
**Carl and Emanuela Magnusson**
MANUFACTURER
**EFM New York, Milan**

These hand-blown glass vases in three different sizes are available in three colors: amethyst, aqua and amber. The concave base is silvered from underneath.

PRODUCT
**"Cleo" Contemporary Crystal Giftware**
DESIGNER
**William E. Hoffer, W E H Design**
MANUFACTURER
**Sasaki**

The "Cleo" vase and bowl are 24 percent lead crystal, hand-crafted in the Japanese style. Available in three sizes: petite, small and large.

PRODUCT
**Sengai Vases and Bowl**
PHOTOGRAPHER
**Andy Spreitzer**

Heavy full-lead crystal Sengai vases have rounded corners and are sandblasted with geometric shapes around the rim.

*Available through Objects by Design.*

PRODUCT
**Handkerchief Vase**
DESIGNER
**Joel Smith**
MANUFACTURER
**Steuben**

A modern interpretation
by Joel Smith of a style
introduced in the early
1930s by Frederick Car-
der, founder of Steuben.
Its spontaneous form
suggests a flourished
handkerchief, giving
it a casual charm.

PRODUCT
**"Irregular Regularities"**
**Vase 2**
DESIGNER
**Deborah Czeresko**
MANUFACTURER
**Deborah Czeresko**

Hand blown and colored glass. Signed and numbered, limited edition of 100.

*Available exclusively through Fullscale Design Gallery, New York.*

PRODUCT
**"Irregular Regularities" Vase**
DESIGNER
**Deborah Czeresko**
MANUFACTURER
**Deborah Czeresko**

Hand blown and colored glass. Signed and numbered, limited edition of 100.

*Available exclusively through Fullscale Design Gallery, New York.*

PRODUCT
**"Irregular Regularities" Glass**
**Collection**
DESIGNER
**Deborah Czeresko**
MANUFACTURER
**Deborah Czeresko**

Hand blown and colored glass. Signed and numbered, limited edition of 100 each.

*Available exclusively through Fullscale Design Gallery, New York.*

PRODUCT
**Ceramic Urns and Bowl**
DESIGNER
**Wesley Dunn**
MANUFACTURER
**Wesley Dunn**
PHOTOGRAPHER
**Errol Hamilton**

Hand thrown ceramic
urns and bowl in vibrant
colors and patterns.

PRODUCT
**Scroll Series**
DESIGNER
**Colleen Zufelt-Tomczak**
MANUFACTURER
**Colleen Zufelt-Tomczak**
PHOTOGRAPHER
**Carson Zullinger**

Wheel thrown whiteware with airbrushed mixed media.

PRODUCT
**Scroll Series**
DESIGNER
**Colleen Zufelt-Tomczak**
MANUFACTURER
**Colleen Zufelt-Tomczak**
PHOTOGRAPHER
**Carson Zullinger**

Wheel thrown vessel with carved lip, airbrushed acrylics, pastels and pencil.

PRODUCT
**The Butterfly Range**
MANUFACTURER
**Belleek**

Gently shaped Belleek
porcelain pieces hand
crafted with skill and attention to detail: vase,
flower pot, salad/fruit
bowl, small covered vase.

PRODUCT
**Alta Mira Vases**
DESIGNER
**Gilbert Portanier**
MANUFACTURER
**Rosenthal, Germany**

Gilbert Portanier's ceramic Alta Mira Vases express painted interpretations of Mediterranean myths, using warm colors and a soft glaze.

*Available through Rosenthal Design Showroom, Dania, Florida*

PRODUCT
**Landscape Vases**
DESIGNER
**Helmut Drexler**
MANUFACTURER
**Rosenthal, Germany**

Made of Rosenthal's Porcelain Noire, a unique porcelain which is black through and through, the *Landscape* vase collection presents a stunning contrast of matte and glossy black porcelain and 24 karat gold.

*Available through Rosenthal Design Showroom, Dania, Florida*

# CHAPTER EIGHT

# Decorative Accessories

*Coffee table vignette, with hand-carved ivory sculpture, designed by Toby Zack.*

*Photo: Dan Forer*

PRODUCT
**Spiked Scent Bottle**
DESIGNER
**Sue L. Amendolara**
MANUFACTURER
**Sue L. Amendolara**
PHOTOGRAPHER
**Rick Potteiger**

Ancient Egyptian and African artwork inspired the design for this spiked scent bottle of sterling silver, ebony and 24 karat gold.

PRODUCT
**Aegyptus Scent Bottle**
DESIGNER
**Sue L. Amendolara**
MANUFACTURER
**Sue L. Amendolara**
PHOTOGRAPHER
**Rick Potteiger**

Sterling silver scent bottle with coral, ebony
and 24 karat gold.
Inspired by ancient
Egyptian art work, the
form suggests the
female figure.

PRODUCT
**Drambuie Decanter**
DESIGNER
**Sue L. Amendolara**
MANUFACTURER
**Sue L. Amendolara**
PHOTOGRAPHER
**Rick Potteiger**

Drambuie Decanter
(10″ × 4″ × 4″) inspired by
ancient Egyptian artwork
and made from sterling
silver, hand-carved slate,
coral and 24 karat gold
foil. The foil is fused to
the surface of the silver
using a Korean tech-
nique—Keum-boo.

PRODUCT
**Bottle**
DESIGNER
**Guido Gambone, Italy**

Glazed ceramic bottle, 1937.

*The Mitchell Wolfson, Jr. Collection*
*Courtesy The Wolfsonian Foundation*
*Miami, Florida*

PRODUCT
**Vessel with Golden Light**
DESIGNER
**Susan Ewing**
**INTERALIA/Design**
MANUFACTURER
**Susan Ewing**
**INTERALIA/Design**
PHOTOGRAPHER
**Rick Potteiger**

Sterling silver and 24
karat vermeil vessel
with lid.

PRODUCT
**"Twelve-Egg" Bowl**
DESIGNER
**Henry Petzal**
MANUFACTURER
**Henry Petzal**

This beautifully designed heavy weight sterling silver bowl was raised from a sheet of 16-gauge sterling, chased from the outside and hammered from the inside.

PRODUCT
**Bowl with Trim**
DESIGNER
**Henry Petzal**
MANUFACTURER
**Henry Petzal**

Sterling silver bowl raised from a 16-gauge sheet. The beading was cast in three pieces and soldered to the edge.

214

PRODUCT
**Eagle, Excalibur**
DESIGNERS
**Donald Pollard/James Houston**
MANUFACTURER
**Steuben**

Donald Pollard's crystal eagle, symbol of liberty. The Excalibur crystal paperweight with removable sterling and 18 karat gold sword/paperknife is inspired by the Arthurian legend.

PRODUCT
**Covered Bowl**
DESIGNER
**Henry Petzal**
MANUFACTURER
**Henry Petzal**

Sterling silver covered bowl with pineapple pattern and lapis lazuli finial.

PRODUCT
**Footed Bowl**
DESIGNER
**Dagobert Peche, Austria**

Glazed earthenware
footed bowl with floral
openwork.

*The Mitchell Wolfson, Jr. Collection*
*Courtesy The Wolfsonian Foundation*
*Miami, Florida*

PRODUCT
**Footed Cone Vase**
DESIGNER
**Ann Morhauser**
MANUFACTURER
**Annieglass Studio, Santa Cruz, California**
PHOTOGRAPHER
**Viktor Budnic**

Limited edition, frosted, sandblasted and gilded cone vase.

PRODUCT
**Azure Blue Bowl**
MANUFACTURER
**Blenko Glass**
PHOTOGRAPHER
**Andy Spreitzer**

Exquisite azure blue bowl of mouth blown West Virginia glass.

*Available through Objects by Design.*

PRODUCT
**Untitled**
DESIGNER
**Marino Moretti**
MANUFACTURER
**Marino Moretti**

Glazed ceramic oval charger.

*Courtesy of Twining Gallery, NYC.*

PRODUCT
**Woman with Harpy**
DESIGNER
**Marino Moretti**
MANUFACTURER
**Marino Moretti**

Handmade and painted ceramic charger with harpy-like half man/half bird motif.

*Courtesy of Twining Gallery, NYC.*

PRODUCT
**"Ibis" Bowl**
MANUFACTURER
**Fulper Pottery Co., USA**

Glazed earthenware bowl
with ibis motif, c. 1912.

*The Mitchell Wolfson, Jr. Collection*
*Courtesy The Wolfsonian Foundation*
*Miami, Florida*

PRODUCT
**Evolution of the Hūmie**
DESIGNER
**Bob Gereke**
MANUFACTURER
**Bob Gereke**
PHOTOGRAPHER
**Bob Gereke**

Stoneware plate series,
thrown and hand painted
with a clear glaze.

PRODUCT
**Limited Edition Pieces**
DESIGNER
**Ann Morhauser**
MANUFACTURER
**Annieglass Studio, Santa Cruz, California**
PHOTOGRAPHER
**Viktor Budnic**

Decorative glass platters and cone vases with colorful glass enamels.

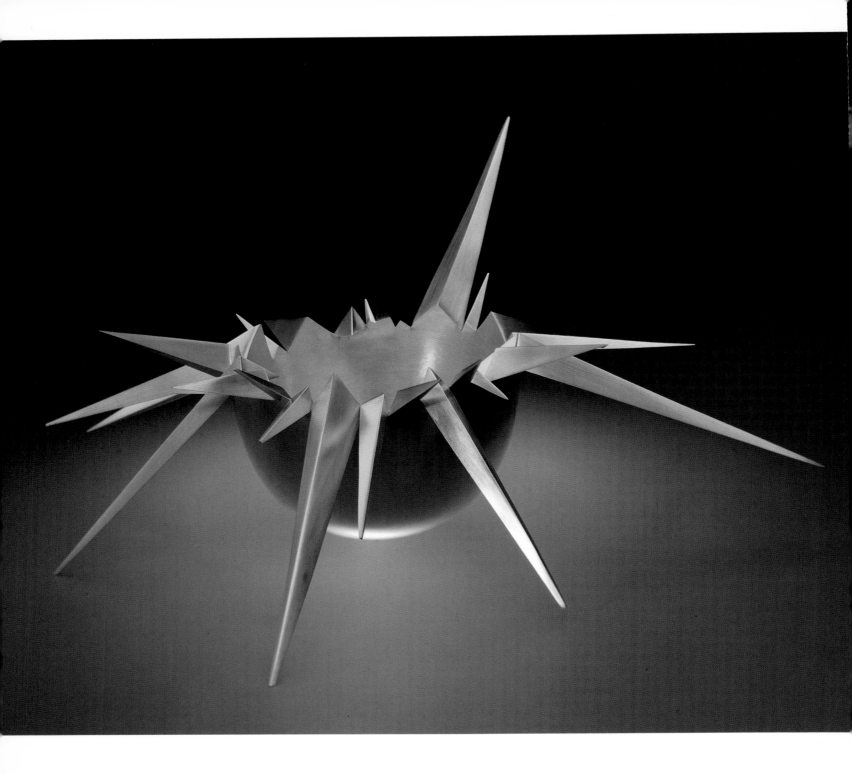

PRODUCT
**Liberty Bowl**
DESIGNER
**Susan Ewing**
**INTERALIA/Design**
MANUFACTURER
**Susan Ewing**
**INTERALIA/Design**
PHOTOGRAPHER
**Rick Potteiger**

Sterling silver bowl.

PRODUCT
**Copper Bowl with Brass Legs**
DESIGNER
**Thomas R. Markusen**
MANUFACTURER
**Thomas R. Markusen**
PHOTOGRAPHER
**Jim Dusen**

Spun copper bowl with
cast brass legs, each in a
different sculptured
form.

PRODUCT
**Animal Anomaly II**
DESIGNER
**Cynthia Eid**
MANUFACTURER
**Cynthia Eid**
PHOTOGRAPHER
**Cynthia Eid**

Sculpture in copper and
sterling.

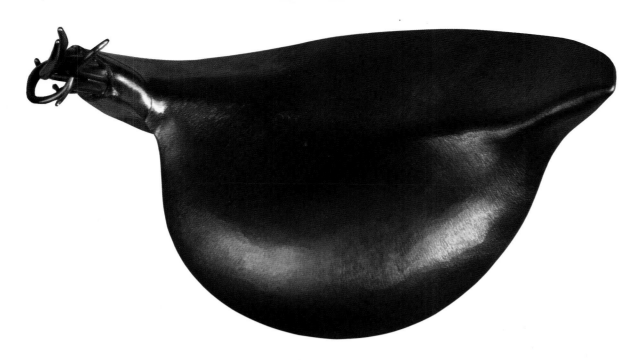

PRODUCT
**Sea-ish II**
DESIGNER
**Cynthia Eid**
MANUFACTURER
**Cynthia Eid**
PHOTOGRAPHER
**Cynthia Eid**

Hand crafted copper container.

PRODUCT
**Sea-ish III**
DESIGNER
**Cynthia Eid**
MANUFACTURER
**Cynthia Eid**
PHOTOGRAPHER
**Cynthia Eid**

Copper container.

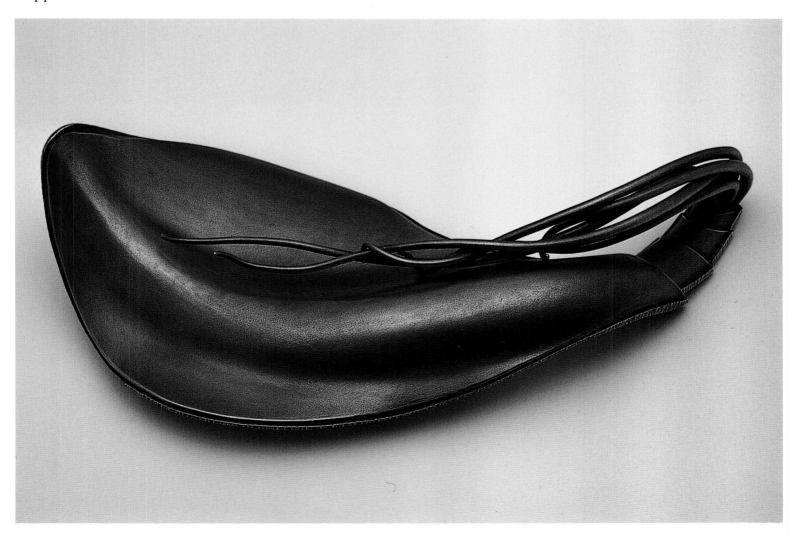

PRODUCT
**Sea-ish II**
DESIGNER
**Cynthia Eid**
MANUFACTURER
**Cynthia Eid**
PHOTOGRAPHER
**Cynthia Eid**

PRODUCT
**Animal Anomaly**
DESIGNER
**Cynthia Eid**
MANUFACTURER
**Cynthia Eid**
PHOTOGRAPHER
**Cynthia Eid**

Sterling silver sculpture.

PRODUCT
**Sugar Bowl**
DESIGNER
**Robert Oppecker**
MANUFACTURER
**Robert Oppecker**
PHOTOGRAPHER
**Robert Oppecker**

Sterling silver sugar
bowl.

*This piece was made possible with a grant
from the Pennsylvania Council on the Arts.*

PRODUCT
**Lidded Container**
DESIGNER
**Robert Oppecker**
MANUFACTURER
**Robert Oppecker**
PHOTOGRAPHER
**Robert Oppecker**

Sterling silver lidded container.

227

PRODUCT
**Container with Malachite Lid**
DESIGNER
**Robert Oppecker**
MANUFACTURER
**Robert Oppecker**
PHOTOGRAPHER
**Lockwood Hoehl**

Sterling silver container
with cut malachite lid.
(2″ × 2″ × 3″) Malachite
cut by Paul Stubbe.

*This piece was made possible with a grant from the Pennsylvania Council on the Arts.*

PRODUCT
**Sterling Box**
DESIGNER
**Harold Rogovin**
MANUFACTURER
**Harold Rogovin**
PHOTOGRAPHER
**Elton Pope-Lance**

Decorative sterling silver
box beautifully accented
with a jade finial. Hand
wrought, hand chased.

PRODUCT
**Book Ends**
DESIGNER
**William Frederick**
MANUFACTURER
**William Frederick**
PHOTOGRAPHER
**William Frederick**

Handsome sterling silver
book ends with ebony
bases.

PRODUCT
**Xylopot**
DESIGNER
**Bob Kopec**
MANUFACTURER
**Bob Kopec**
PHOTOGRAPHER
**Steve Plotnick**

Lathe-turned, hand
sculpted wooden vessel
of walnut, zebrano and
maple.

PRODUCT
**Xylopot**
DESIGNER
**Bob Kopec**
MANUFACTURER
**Bob Kopec**
PHOTOGRAPHER
**Steve Plotnick**

Maple, walnut and oak
are beautifully integrated
in this lathe-turned, hand
sculpted wooden vessel.

PRODUCT
**Scatola**
DESIGNER
**C&E Magnusson**
MANUFACTURER
**EFM New York, Milan**

Solid Swiss pearwood
sliding top box.

PRODUCT
**Brass Box**
DESIGNER
**Roberta Masur-Maxfield**
MANUFACTURER
**Roberta Masur-Maxfield**
PHOTOGRAPHER
**Lynda LaRoche**

structed brass box
rushed finish.

PRODUCT
**Bowl**
DESIGNER
**Mark Gillen: OTO**
MANUFACTURER
**Mark Gillen: OTO**
PHOTOGRAPHER
**Yoshiko Ebihara**

Beautifully formed, this hand carved marble bowl makes an outstanding centerpiece.

*Available through Gallery 91, New York.*

PRODUCT
**Bowl**
DESIGNER
**Mark Gillen: OTO**
MANUFACTURER
**Mark Gillen: OTO**
PHOTOGRAPHER -
**Yoshiko Ebihara**

Hand carved marble bowl with jagged lip.

*Available through Gallery 91, New York.*

PRODUCT
**Wire Vessel**
DESIGNER
**Susan Steinberg**
MANUFACTURER
**Susan Steinberg**
PHOTOGRAPHER
**William H. Sanders**

Handmade wire vessel.
Dark annealed steel shell
with triangular alumi-
num and copper. Natural
and patina finish.

*Available through Hoffman Gallery, Fort
Lauderdale, Florida.*

PRODUCT
**Wire Vessel**
DESIGNER
**Susan Steinberg**
MANUFACTURER
**Susan Steinberg**
PHOTOGRAPHER
**William H. Sanders**

Wire vessel handmade
from a variety of non-
ferrous wire, including
recycled/surplus mate-
rials. Metals used are
copper, aluminum, red
and yellow brass, with a
finish combining natural
and patina.

*Available through Hoffman Gallery, Fort
Lauderdale, Florida.*

Cons
with b

PRODUCT
**Wire Vessel**
DESIGNER
**Susan Steinberg**
MANUFACTURER
**Susan Steinberg**
PHOTOGRAPHER
**William H. Sanders**

Handmade wire vessel.
Brass and aluminum
shell with copper. Natu-
ral and patina finish.

*Available through Hoffman Gallery, Fort
Lauderdale, Florida.*

# APPENDIX

Al Evans Interiors, Inc.
P.O. Box 2037
Miami Beach, FL 33140

Amendolara, Sue L.
98 Chestnut St.
Edinburgh, PA 16419

Anderson/Schwartz Architects
40 Hudson Street
New York, NY 10013

Annieglass Studio
303 Potrero St. #8
Santa Cruz, CA 95060

Banner Studio Inc.
Box 217
Griswold Rd.
Monterey, MA 01245

Bissell & Wilhite Co.
8306 Wilshire Blvd.
Suite 39
Beverly Hills, CA 90211

Cartier Inc.
2 E. 52nd Street
New York, NY 10022

Cecula, Marek
105 Sullivan St.
New York, NY 10012

Crystallery de Genesis
P.O. Box 19559
Rochester, NY 14619

Dansk International Designs, Ltd.
Radio Circle Rd.
Mt. Kisco, NY 10549

Douglas Design Office
Shibuya-Ku
Kamiyama-Cho 12-7
Uchino Heights #201
Tokyo-Japan

E F M
568 Broadway
New York, NY 10012

Frederick, William
1858 N. Sedgwick St.
Chicago, IL 60614

Fullscale Design Gallery
151 First Ave. Suite 211
New York, NY 10003

Gallery 91
91 Grand St.
New York, NY 10013

Gorham, Inc.
P.O. Box 6150
Providence, RI 02940

Grainware
2600 N. Pulaski Rd.
Chicago, IL 60639-2197

Grigsby, Ann E.
315 Crockett St.
Seattle, WA 98109

Interalia Design
P.O. Box 404
Oxford, OH 45056

Jason McCoy, Inc.
41 E. 57th St.
New York, NY 10022

Kopec, Bob
715 Raven Ave.
Longwood, FL 32750

LaFollette, Curtis K.
R.R.1 Box 443
Harrington, ME 04643

Lax, Michael
124 E. 65th St.
New York, NY 10021

Lenox, Inc.
100 Lenox Dr.
Lawrenceville, NJ 08648

Lewis Dolin Inc.
588 Broadway
New York, NY 10012

Lovegrove, Ross
Studio X
81 Southern Row
London W1D 5AL

Luyk, Ton
412-415 Viscaya Ave.
Coral Gables, FL 33134

Markusen, Thomas R.
17218 Roosevelt Hwy.
Kendall, NY 14476

Masur-Maxfield, Roberta
461 W. Hillcrest
Dekalb, IL 60115

McGuckian, Floria Popovici
105 Wall St.
Rockville, MD 20850

Mindscape Gallery
1506 Sherman Ave.
Evanston, IL 60201

National Tabletop Association
355 Lexington Ave.
New York, NY 10017-6603

Nichols, Robyn
2000 Grand Ave.
Kansas City, MO 64108

Objects By Design
208 Farwood Rd.
Wynnewood, PA 19096

Oggetti
48 NW 25th St.
Miami, FL 33127

Oppecker, Robert
925 Ebert Road
Coopersburg, PA 18036

Pearson, Ronald Hayes
RR1 Box 158
Old Ferry Road
Deer Isle, ME 04627

Petzal, Henry
5050 LaJolla Blvd. P-C
San Diego, CA 92109

Reed & Barton
144 W. Britannia St.
Taunton, MA 02780

Richard Plumer Design
155 NE 40th St.
Miami, FL 33137

Rogovin, Harold
P.O. Box 251
Califon, NJ 07830

Romulus Craft
HCR 21 Box 85
Route 110
Washington, VT 05675

Rosenthal Design Showroom
1855 Griffin Rd. Ste-B408
Dania, FL 33004

Royal Copenhagen
27 Holland Ave.
White Plains, NY 10603

Royal Worcester
Royal China & Porcelain Companies Inc.
1265 Glen Ave.
Morristown, NJ 08057

Royston, Michel
Route 2, Box 613
Hat Creek, CA 96040

Saenger Porcelain
18 Mimosa Dr.
Newark, DE 19711

Sasaki Inc.
41 Madison Ave.
Morristown, NY 10010

Society of American Silversmiths
P.O. Box 3599
Cranston, RI 02910

Spode
Royal China & Porcelain Companies Inc.
1265 Glen Ave.
Morristown, NJ 08057

Steinberg, Susan
784 Middle River Dr.
Ft. Lauderdale, FL 33304

Steuben/Corning
717 Fifth Ave.
New York, NY 10022

Stilnovo
370 Altara Ave.
Coral Gables, FL 33140

Stromsoe Studios
2410 Langton St.
Cambria, CA 93428

Tiffany & Company
727 Fifth Ave.
New York, NY 10022

Twining Gallery
568 Broadway
New York, NY 10012

Villeroy & Boch Tableware
41 Madison Ave.
New York, NY 10011

W E H Design
1908 Yardley Rd.
Yardley, PA 19067

The Wolfsonian Foundation
1001 Washington Ave.
Miami Beach, FL 33139

Zufelt-Tomczak, Colleen
736 E. 6th St.
Wilmington, DE 19801

# INDEX

## Designers

## Manufacturers